TRUMPTRUMP

Modern Day Presidential

JANUARY 20 - JULY 21, 2017

WARREN CRAGHEAD III

RETROFIT COMICS
BIG PLANET COMICS

For A.W., V.C.-W. and G.C.-W.
I'm sorry this is still happening.

TRUMPTRUMP modern day presidential is ©2018 Warren Craghead

This work originally published at trumptrump.biz
More at craghead.com

Thanks to J.S. and B.B.

Retrofit 77

ISBN 978-1-940398-83-9

Published by Retrofit Comics & Big Planet Comics
Washington, D.C.
retrofitcomics.com /// bigplanetcomics.com

Printed in Canada

Drawing Donald Trump as president is different than drawing him as a candidate or the president-elect. When I started drawing these daily grotesque portraits of Trump (in July 2016, when he accepted the Republican nomination for president) one of my goals was to make it hard for people supporting him to look away from his horror.

By drawing Trump as president, in addition to warning people away from him, I try to document what he is doing to our government, our politics and us. What is happening is not normal and I want, in a small way, to try to resist normalizing Trump, his minions and their schemes. This book's title, "modern day presidential," is taken from a Trump quote (drawn on page 177) and, unfortunately, he's not far off in seeing himself as a terrible trailblazer.

This book collects daily drawings of the first six months of the Trump Administration, starting at his inauguration in January 2017. During that time, among other awful things, Trump issued a travel ban from Muslim-majority countries, pushed Republicans in Congress to try to kill the Affordable Care Act, and chafed under the investigations into foreign meddling in the 2016 presidential election and, specifically, Russian collusion with his campaign.

The way I drew Trump changed over time too. The book starts with him as a hunk of meat in a blasted landscape, orbited by minions like Sean Spicer, Kellyanne Conway and Steve Bannon. Trump became a pathetic jester-prince, then later he and his cronies melt into Goya-esque loose-drawn monsters. Near the end of the book I drew him in four-panel comics, adding simple narratives to the project. Characters wander in the drawings with pizzas and guns and bones. Bear arms loom and claw. Fires burn.

All along I looked at (and stole from) artists like Philip Guston, Kathe Kollwitz, Saul Steinberg, Pablo Picasso, Otto Dix and others to find ways to show Trump and the monsters he and his administration are. Thanks to them, and especially to Jared Smith of Retrofit Comics for encouraging and publishing this collection.

I've continued to draw Trump - you can see the work daily at trumptrump.biz.

For all our sakes, I hope I can stop drawing this terror soon.

— Warren Craghead III, September 2018

"This is your day. This is your celebration. And this, the United States of America, is your country."

Inauguration Day.

"Watched protests yesterday but was under the impression that we just had an election! Why didn't these people vote? Celebs hurt cause badly."

The Women's March on Washington drew 500,000 to 1,000,000 people to protest the incoming Trump Administration.

"You're saying it's a falsehood. And they're giving – Sean Spicer, our press secretary – gave alternative facts."

Trump Senior Advisor Kellyanne Conway, commenting on White House Spokesman Sean Spicer's lie about the size of the inauguration crowd ("...this was the largest audience to ever witness an inauguration, period.")

Trump advisor Kellyanne Conway: "And it's really time for him to put in his own security intelligence community."

Trump at the CIA: "So I only like to say that because I love honesty. I like honest reporting. I will tell you the final time: although I will say it, when you let in your thousands of other people that had been trying to come in, because I am coming back. We may have to get you a larger room. [laughter, applause] We may have to get you a larger room. ...

I just wanted to really say that I love you. I respect you. There's nobody that I respect more. You're going to do a fantastic job. And we're going to start winning again. And you're going to be leading the charge."

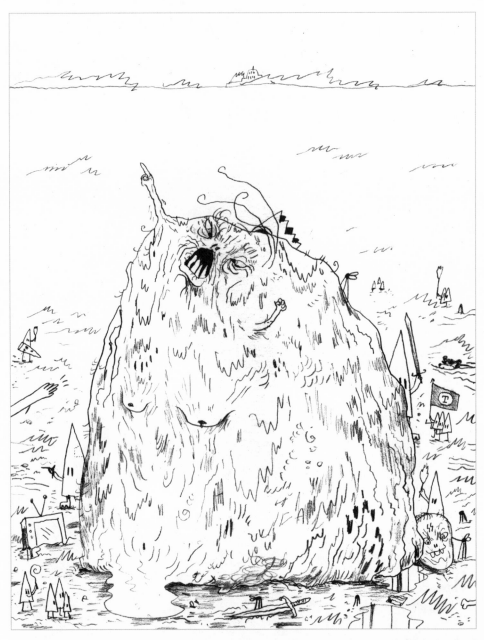

"But you know, we have something that's amazing because, we had, it looked honestly, it looked like a million and a half people. Whatever it was. But it went all the way back to the Washington Monument.

"Now that's not bad. But it's a lie. We had 250,000 people literally around, you know, the little bowl that we constructed. That was 250,000 people. The rest of the 20 block area all the way back to the Washington Monument was packed.

"So we caught them. And we caught them in a beauty. And I think they're going to pay a big price"

Trump is upset about the crowd size at his inauguration.

"I got a standing ovation. In fact, they said it was the biggest standing ovation since Peyton Manning had won the Super Bowl and they said it was equal. I got a standing ovation. It lasted for a long period of time."

"I'm gonna be the president of a safe country."

Trump used executive orders to ban temporarily ban refugees from seven Muslim-majority countries. Nations he has business dealings with are not part of this list.

His orders attempt to ban refugees fleeing Syria's civil war, and would have drastically lowered the number of refugees the U.S. would accept. Christians would be prioritized to come to the U.S. as refugees. Others would be subject to unspecified "extreme vetting."

Trump advisor Steve Bannon:

"The media here is the opposition party. They don't understand this country. They still do not understand why Donald Trump is the president of the United States..."

"You're the opposition party. Not the Democratic Party. You're the opposition party. The media's the opposition party."

In his first week as President Trump signed executive orders:
- Barring immigration and refugees from seven Muslim-majority countries
- Instructing federal agencies to weaken Obamacare
- Pushing the Keystone oil pipeline (which he has a financial interest in)
- Reinstating a ban on international abortion counseling
- Weakening Obamacare

*The turtle is Senate Majority Leader Mitch McConnell; the vampire head is
Speaker of the House Paul Ryan. Vice-President Mike Pence is on top of
Trump.*

"But I have spoken as recently as 24 hours ago with people at the highest level of intelligence. And I asked them the question, "Does it work? Does torture work?" And the answer was, "Yes, absolutely."

"I wanna do everything within the bounds of what you're allowed to do legally. But do I feel it works? Absolutely I feel it works. Have I spoken to people at the top levels and people that have seen it work? I haven't seen it work. But I think it works."

"Darkness is good. Dick Cheney. Darth Vader. Satan. That's power."

Quote from alt-right guru Steve Bannon, who Trump put on the National Security Council while removing the chair of the Joint Chiefs and the Director of National Intelligence.

Trump's Muslim ban was orchestrated by advisors Steve Bannon and Stephen Miller, who have a long history of promoting Islamophobia, courting anti-Muslim extremists, and boosting white nationalists.

Trump nominates Neil Gorsuch to fill the vacant seat on the U.S. Supreme Court. Gorsuch is a conservative judge who idolized the late Justice Scalia.

President Obama's nominee to the Supreme Court, Merrick Garland, was blocked by Senate Republicans and was denied a hearing or a vote.

The ghost of Justice Scalia is on Gorsuch. McConnell looks on happily, driving a knife into the Constitution and a garland. Trump's large adult sons are also there.

On a phone call to the prime minister of Australia, Trump said, "...this was the worst call by far" and abruptly hung up on him. On a call to the president of Mexico Trump said, "You have a bunch of bad hombres down there. You aren't doing enough to stop them. I think your military is scared. Our military isn't, so I just might send them down to take care of it."

Trump, doing Bannon's bidding, is rolling over his chief of staff Reince Priebus, the former Republican National Committee chair.

"We expect to be cutting a lot out of Dodd-Frank because, frankly, I have so many people, friends of mine, who have nice businesses who can't borrow money. They just can't get any money because the banks just won't let them borrow, because of the rules and regulations in Dodd-Frank..."

The Dodd-Frank Wall Street Reform and Consumer Protection Act was passed in response to the 2008 global financial crisis and brought significant changes to financial regulation to improve stability and consumer protection.

"The opinion of this so-called judge, which essentially takes law-enforcement away from our country, is ridiculous and will be overturned!"

Trump upset about his travel ban being challenged.

BILL O'REILLY: But he's a killer though. Putin's a killer.

TRUMP: There are a lot of killers. We've got a lot of killers. What do you think — our country's so innocent. You think our country's so innocent?

Stacking up on Trump: Bannon, Trump advisor Stephen Miller, and National Security Advisor Michael Flynn.

"I call my own shots, largely based on an accumulation of data, and everyone knows it. Some FAKE NEWS media, in order to marginalize, lies!"

Bannon under the bed.

Betsy DeVos is confirmed as Secretary of the Department of Education, despite a lack of experience and deep questions about her corrupting political donations.

Pence is lurking behind her. See note on page 195 for a list of her family's political donations.

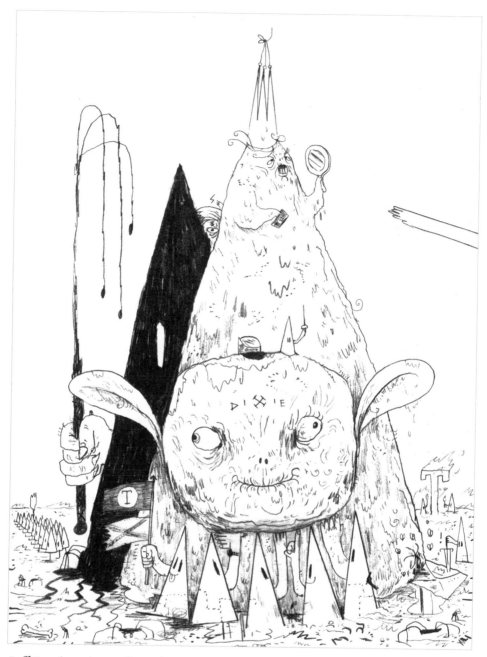

Jeff Sessions is confirmed as Attorney General.

Sen. Elizabeth Warren is silenced and censured for reading a letter sent to the Senate by Coretta Scott King, widow of Martin Luther King, Jr., which denounces Sessions as a racist.

Thomas H. Figures, a black Assistant U.S. Attorney who worked under Sessions, told the committee that Sessions said he thought the Ku Klux Klan was okay until he learned its members smoked marijuana. Sessions had summoned Figures to his office and admonished him to "be careful what you say to white folks."

"SEE YOU IN COURT, THE SECURITY OF OUR NATION IS AT STAKE!"

Trump reacting to a court stopping his travel ban.

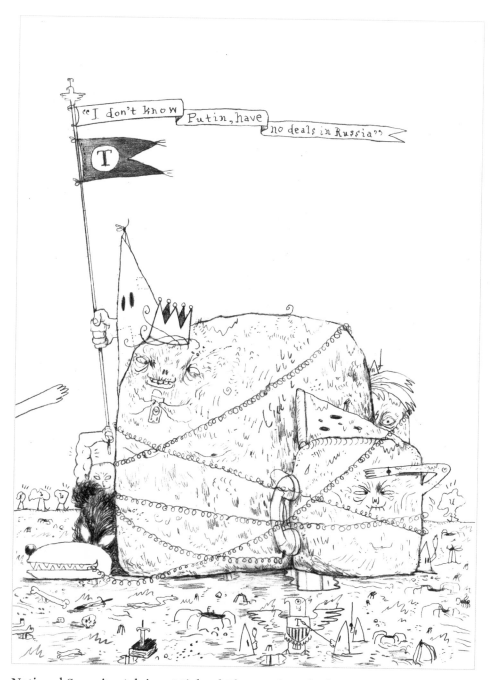

National Security Advisor Michael Flynn privately discussed U.S. sanctions against Russia with that country's ambassador to the United States during the month before President Trump took office, contrary to public assertions by Trump officials.

"Usually around 6:30 p.m., or sometimes later, Mr. Trump retires upstairs to the residence to recharge, vent and intermittently use Twitter. ...When Mr. Trump is not watching television in his bathrobe or on his phone reaching out to old campaign hands and advisers, he will sometimes set off to explore the unfamiliar surroundings of his new home."

From an article in the New York Times by Glenn Thrush and Maggie Haberman

Trump advisor Stephen Miller on ABC News' This Week:

STEPHANOPOULOS: – just for the record, you have provided absolutely no evidence. The president's made a statement.

MILLER: The White House has provided enormous evidence with respect to voter fraud, with respect to people being registered in more than one state, dead people voting, non-citizens being registered to vote. George, it is a fact and you will not deny it, that there are massive numbers of non-citizens in this country, who are registered to vote. That is a scandal.

We should stop the presses. And as a country, we should be aghast about the fact that you have people who have no right to vote in this country, registered to vote, canceling out the franchise of lawful citizens of this country. That's the story we should be talking about. And I'm prepared to go on any show, anywhere, anytime, and repeat it and say the President of the United States is correct 100 percent.

Michael T. Flynn, Trump's national security advisor, resigned after it was revealed that he had questionable conversations with the Russian ambassador to the United States and had allegedly misled Vice President Mike Pence and other top White House officials.

Trump, with Bannon and Miller, turns his back on Flynn.

Trump senior advisor Stephen Miller on Face The Nation:
"...our opponents, the media and the whole world will soon see as we begin to take further actions, that the powers of the president to protect our country are very substantial and will not be questioned."

Trump's reaction to his talk show appearances:
"Congratulations Stephen Miller- on representing me this morning on the various Sunday morning shows. Great job!"

"The leaks are absolutely real, the news is fake, because so much of the news is fake."

See note on page 196 for more from this press conference.

"The fake news media is going crazy with their conspiracy theories and blind hatred. @MSNBC & @CNN are unwatchable. @foxandfriends is great!"

"This Russian connection non-sense is merely an attempt to cover-up the many mistakes made in Hillary Clinton's losing campaign."

"Information is being illegally given to the failing @nytimes & @washingtonpost by the intelligence community (NSA and FBI?).Just like Russia"

Pro-Russia Trump cronies Paul Manafort and Carter Page in the back right. The former Soviet republics Estonia, Lithuania, Latvia and Ukraine scared In the front. Putin on top of it all.

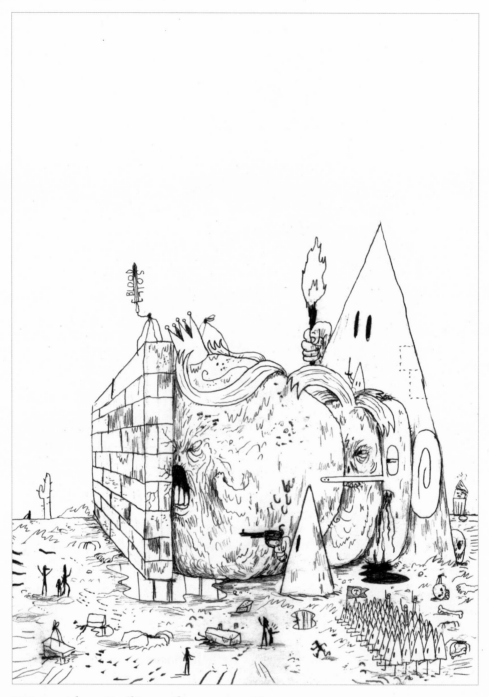

"We must keep "evil" out of our country!"

Trump's three weekend trips (out of four as president) to his "Southern White House" Mar-a-Lago have cost U.S. taxpayers $10 million. A portion of that goes back to Trump's businesses - he owns Mar-a-Lago.

Don Jr. and Eric Trump lurking in the back right.

Because Trump's wife and son continue to live in New York the city is paying $500,000 a day to guard Trump Tower, according to police officials' estimates, an amount that could reach $183 million a year. Some of that money flows to Trump as rental fees the Secret Service pays for space in Trump Tower.

The Secret Service and U.S. embassy staff paid nearly $100,000 in hotel room bills to support Eric Trump's trip to promote a Trump-brand condo tower in Uruguay. Both of Trump's adult sons recently traveled to Dubai to open a Trump gold course, again with taxpayer-supported security and logistics.

The older Trump sons in the front left, Trump's wife and younger son at Trump Tower in the back.

A group of Trump operatives, including top lawyer Michael Cohen (bottom left), Felix Sater (bottom right) and pro-Putin Ukrainian parliamentarian Andriy V. Artemenko (middle) are pushing President Trump on a 'peace plan' for Russia and Ukraine masterminded by Vladimir Putin.

Sater, a Russian emigrant, was key to channeling Russian capital to Trump for years. Sater is also a multiple felon and at least a one-time FBI informant.

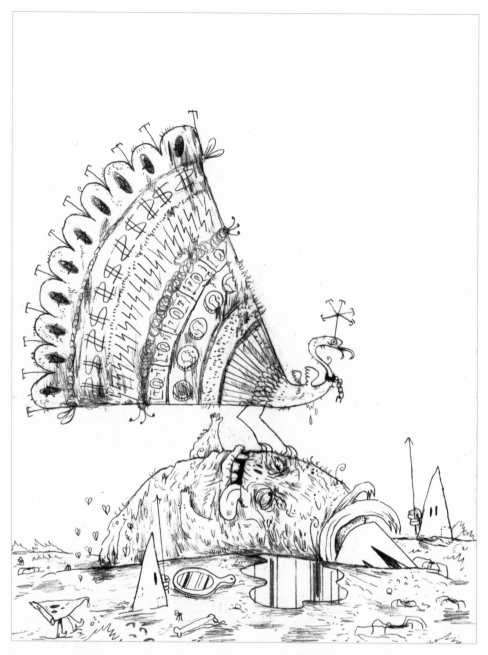

"I'm a person that very strongly believes in academics. In fact, every time I say, I had an uncle who was a great professor at MIT for 35 years, who did a fantastic job in so many different ways academically. He was an academic genius."

"And then they say: 'is Donald Trump an intellectual?' Trust me. I'm like a smart person."

Trump signs executive order rolling back protections for transgender students.

"The FAKE NEWS media (failing @nytimes, @CNN, @NBCNews and many more) is not my enemy, it is the enemy of the American people. SICK!"

Arm with lamp in front left from "Guernica" by Picasso.

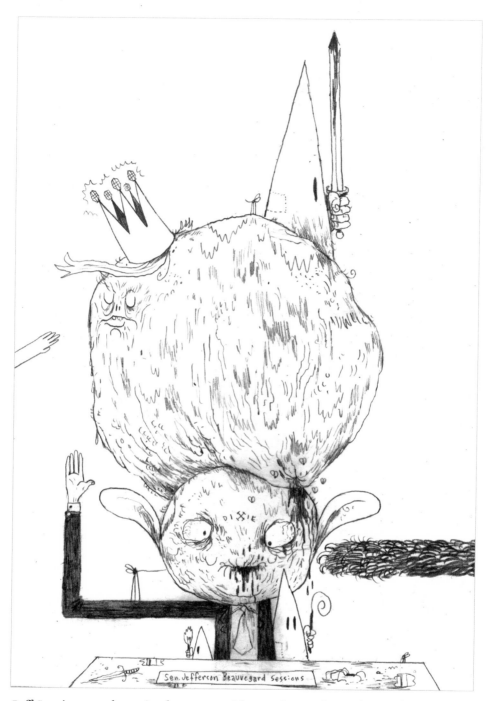

Jeff Sessions spoke twice last year with Russia's ambassador to the United States which he lied about when asked about possible contacts between members of President Trump's campaign and representatives of Moscow during Sessions's confirmation hearing to become attorney general.

"I will not be attending the White House Correspondents' Association Dinner this year. Please wish everyone well and have a great evening!"

"Thank you for the great rallies all across the country. Tremendous support. Make America Great Again!"

The Trump Administration has "unshackled" ICE immigration and Border Patrol officers, leading to militarized and newly emboldened agents to arrest people as they drop their kids at schools and outside churches and to "check papers" on domestic flights.

LIVE DRAW OF TRUMP'S FEBRUARY 28 ADDRESS TO CONGRESS

Pence and Ryan

It's Trump. Ugh

Pressing flesh

KEEP CLAPPING MINIONS

YAY

Our beautiful leader

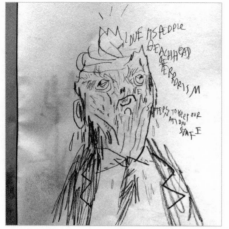

TRUMP

I AM TALKING

REPUBLICANZ

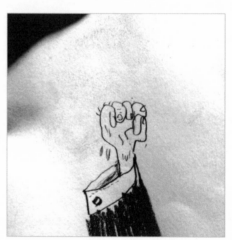

His hands really are tiny.

I want to gut public schools NOW CLAP FOR ME

I'm making a government immigrant hate org! YAY!

I LOVE WHEN CLAPS ARE FOR ME

No more trivial fights (gestures towards Democrats)

I did good I DID GOOD MAGA

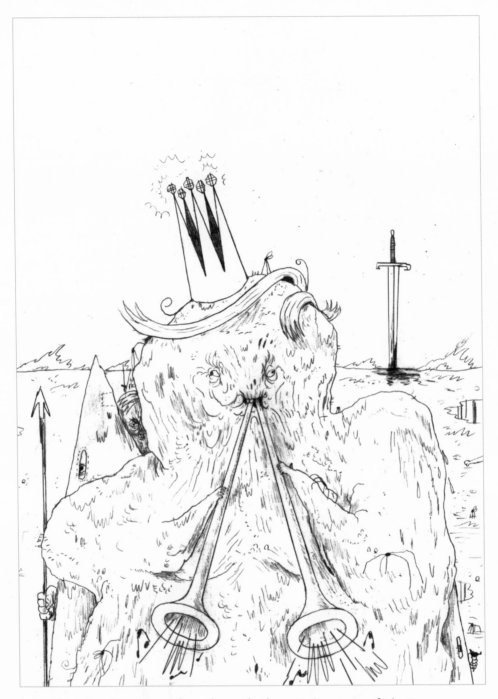

"Terrible! Just found out that Obama had my "wires tapped" in Trump Tower just before the victory. Nothing found. This is McCarthyism!"

Since Trump has been President, the Republicans have introduced many bills, including ones to eliminate the Environmental Protection Agency and the Department of Education, to defund Planned Parenthood, weaken unions and attack abortion rights.

Pence, Paul Ryan and Priebus dancing for joy. McConnell is a turtle. See note on page 196 for a list of bills. Drawing based on a print by Picasso.

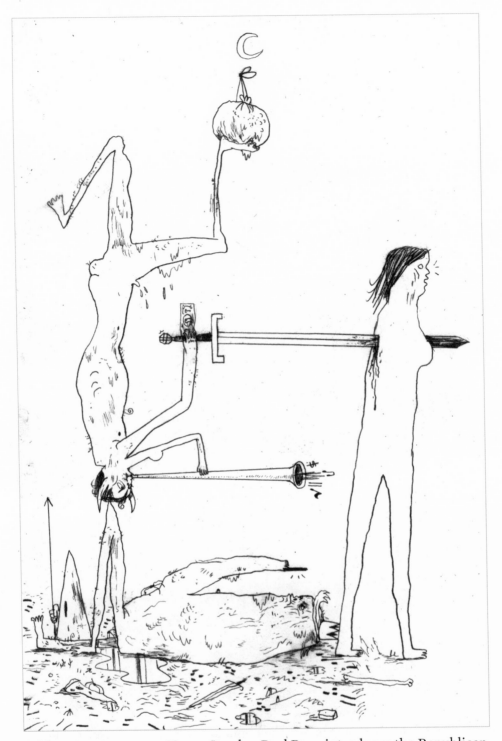

With Trump's support, House Speaker Paul Ryan introduces the Republican anti-Obamacare health bill which lowers taxes on the wealthy and makes health care more expensive and less accessible for lower and middle class Americans.

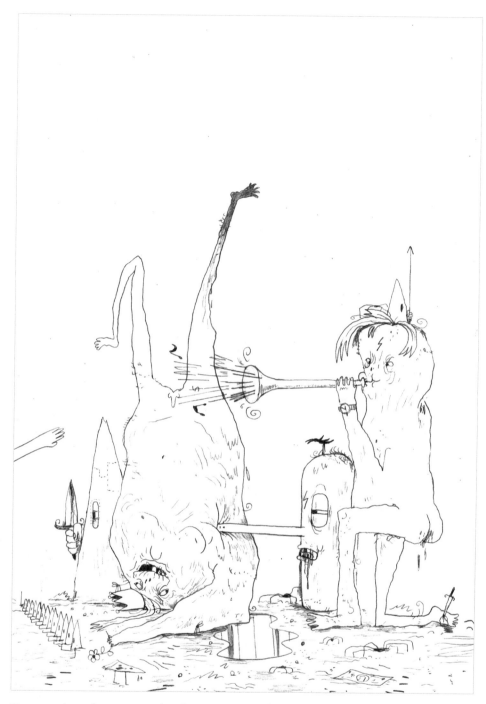

Trump signed a new, revised executive order on immigration, suspending immigration into the United States from six predominantly Muslim countries.

Miller and Bannon again. This drawing is very generous to Bannon's physique.

"On International Women's Day, join me in honoring the critical role of women here in America & around the world."

"I have tremendous respect for women and the many roles they serve that are vital to the fabric of our society and our economy."

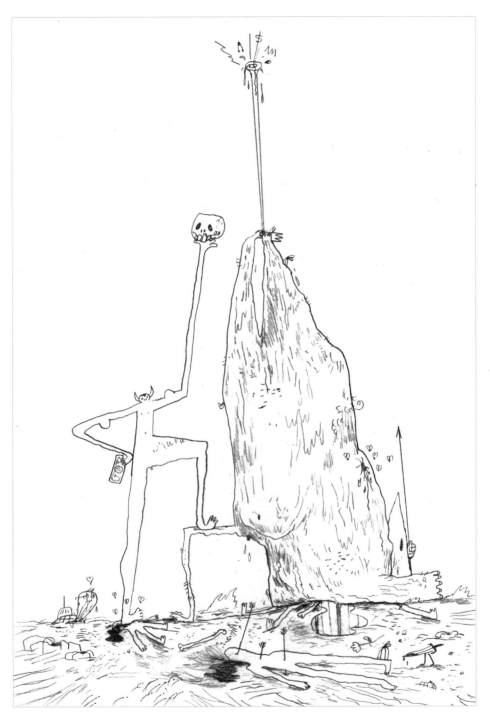

"Despite what you hear in the press, healthcare is coming along great. We are talking to many groups and it will end in a beautiful picture!"

Ryan and McConnell prepping to kill Obamacare.

Trump Spokesman Sean Spicer in a press briefing:

REPORTER: "In the past, the president has referred to particular job reports as phony or totally fiction. Does the president believe that this jobs report was accurate and a fair way to measure the economy?"

SPICER: "I talked to the president prior to this, and he said to quote him very clearly. They may have been phony in the past, but it's very real now."

"Does anybody really believe that a reporter, who nobody ever heard of, "went to his mailbox" and found my tax returns? @NBCNews FAKE NEWS!"

Trump sitting on Spicer.

"This will be a plan where you can choose your doctor, and this will be a plan where you can choose your plan. And you know what the plan is. This is the plan. It's a complicated process, but actually it's very simple, it's called good health care."

Paul Ryan working to kill Obamacare.

"A judge has just blocked our executive order on travel and refugees coming in to our country from certain countries. The order blocked was a watered-down version of the first order. This ruling makes us look weak, which we no longer are."

"It's time for us to embrace our glorious national destiny."

Trump spends his seventh consecutive weekend at a Trump property - his fifth at Mar-a-Lago in Palm Beach, Florida. Each Florida weekend costs the U.S. taxpayers $3 million, some of which goes into payments to Trump's businesses.

Trump Budget Director Mick Mulvaney at a press conference about a proposed budget that cuts funding for most social programs, including Meals on Wheels:

MULVANEY: No, I don't think so. In fact, I think it's—I think it's probably one of the most compassionate things we can do to actually—you're—

REPORTER: Cut programs that help the elderly and kids?

MULVANEY: You're only focusing on half of the equation, right? You're focusing on recipients of the money. We're trying to focus on both the recipients of the money and the folks who give us the money in the first place. And I think it's fairly compassionate to go to them and say, "Look, we're not going to ask you for your hard-earned money anymore."

"Moments ago, I learned that a district judge in Hawaii... (BOOING) ...part of the much overturned 9th Circuit Court... (BOOING) ...and I have to be nice. Otherwise I'll get criticized for... (APPLAUSE) ...for speaking poorly about our courts. I'll be – I'll be criticized by these people, among the most dishonest people in the world. (APPLAUSE) I will be criticized... (BOOING) (APPLAUSE) ...I'll be criticized by them for speaking harshly about our courts. I would never want to do that..."

Drawn from a Picasso bullfight drawing.

The Ryan/Trump Obamacare repeal bill, under the guise of repealing Obamacare, also guts Medicaid, which many older Americans count on for help with nursing home expenses.

Neil Gorsuch, Trump's Supreme Court nominee and acolyte of the late Justice Scalia, evaded answering questions in his Senate confirmation hearing.

A knife through a garland.

The House votes on the "American Health Care Act," which would repeal Obamacare, give wealthy Americans a huge tax break, gut Medicare and Medicaid and cause 24 million Americans to lose their health insurance.

Ryan trying hard to kill Obamacare.

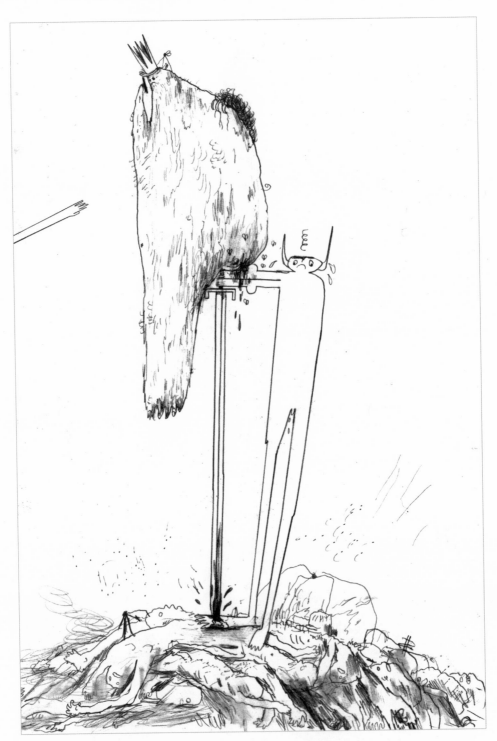

Despite Trump's "deal making" expertise, the AHCA, a Republican bill to repeal Obamacare with a mix of tax cuts for the wealthy and cuts to Medicare and Medicaid, fails in the Republican-controlled House.

Ryan fails, stabs himself in the foot.

"I'm not betrayed. They're friends of mine. I'm disappointed. I'm a little surprised, to be honest with you. It was pretty much there within grasp."

Trump whining about the failure of the Republican health-care bill.

REPORTER: "...traditionally people in your position in the Oval Office have not said things unless they can verify they are true."

TRUMP: "Well, I'm not, well, I think, I'm not saying, I'm quoting, Michael, I'm quoting highly respected people and sources from major television networks."

"I'm a very instinctual person, but my instinct turns out to be right. Hey, look, in the meantime, I guess I can't be doing so badly, because I'm President, and you're not."

"If the people of our great country could only see how viciously and inaccurately my administration is covered by certain media!"

"The country believes me. Hey. I went to Kentucky two nights ago, we had 25,000 people in a massive basketball arena. There wasn't a seat, they had to send away people. I went to Tennessee four nights ago. We had a packed house, they had to send away thousands of people. You saw that, right. Did you see that?"

Trump's son-in-law and senior advisor is tasked with leading an "innovation" office at the White House. Despite earlier statements to the contrary, Trump's daughter Ivanka is moving into a West Wing office and obtaining security clearance.

Sebastian Gorka, Trump's top counter-terrorism adviser, is a formal member of a Hungarian far-right group that is listed by the U.S. State Department as having been "under the direction of the Nazi Government of Germany" during World War II.

Gorka also wears a medal associated with a Nazi ally who oversaw the deportation of thousands of Jews during WWII.

Vice President Mike Pence casts the tie-breaking vote in the Senate to give states permission to withhold federal family planning funds from Planned Parenthood and other abortion providers.

"When will Sleepy Eyes Chuck Todd and @NBCNews start talking about the Obama SURVEILLANCE SCANDAL and stop with the Fake Trump/ Russia story?"

"Anybody (especially Fake News media) who thinks that Repeal & Replace of ObamaCare is dead does not know the love and strength in R Party!"

"Now that Obama's poll numbers are in tailspin – watch for him to launch a strike in Libya or Iran. He is desperate."

A Trump tweet from 2012. Trump launched a strike in Syria when his poll numbers stayed low.

"Uh, we're working on health care. Can I just say, so when you called the health care bill, you know, that was just a negotiation. You didn't hear me say it's over. That was a negotiation. You understand? A continuing negotiation. It may go on for a long time or it may go on until this afternoon. I don't know. It's a continuing negotiation."

"Big increase in traffic into our country from certain areas, while our people are far more vulnerable, as we wait for what should be EASY D!"

About Fox News personality Bill O'Reilly who has been accused by many women of sexual assault:

TRUMP: I think he's a person I know well. He's a good person. I think he may, you know, I think he shouldn't have settled, personally, I think he shouldn't have settled.

REPORTER: How come?

TRUMP: Because you — should have taken it all the way. No, I know Bill. Bill's a good person.

REPORTER: Yeah.

TRUMP: I don't think Bill would do anything wrong.

"It's been very much misreported that we failed with health care. We haven't failed with health care; we're negotiating, and we continue to negotiate."

"One by one we are keeping our promises - on the border, on energy, on jobs, on regulations. Big changes are happening!"

"Jobs are returning, illegal immigration is plummeting, law, order and justice are being restored. We are truly making America great again!"

"North Korea is looking for trouble. If China decides to help, that would be great. If not, we will solve the problem without them! U.S.A."

"And I joked that day — I said, can you imagine the head of this big Canadian company, in this case, they build pipelines — and they failed. Didn't work. They paid millions and millions and hundreds of millions of dollars to consultants and lawyers, and they failed. And it was over. And then one day Trump wins, and a few days later they get a knock on the door — sir, the Keystone pipeline was just approved."

"I've shaken them up, and I think we've had one of the most successful 13 weeks in the history of Presidents."

Trump's Supreme Court pick Neil Gorsuch is confirmed by the Senate after unprecedented rule changes on the vote.

McConnell, the ghost of Scalia and the hidden hand of rich conservatives are all supporting Gorsuch.

Trump launches a military strike against Syria.

Trump was, once again, playing golf.

Neil Gorsuch is sworn in to the Supreme Court.

TRUMP: "I especially want to express our gratitude to Senator Mitch McConnell for all that he did to make this achievement possible. So, thank you, Mitch." (Applause.)

President Donald Trump on Saturday night had a friendly chat at his Mar-a-Lago resort in Palm Beach with twin conservative mega-donor brothers David and Bill Koch, whose family had clashed with Trump during the campaign.

"I always assume no Democrat votes. Now, the good thing is we have the House. We have the Senate. And we have the White House. So we're all set."

CNBC HOST MARIA BARTIROMO: You redirected Navy ships to go toward the Korean Peninsula. What we are doing right now in terms of North Korea?

TRUMP: You never know, do you? You never know.

BARTIROMO: That's all (INAUDIBLE)...

TRUMP: You know I don't think about the military.

Full quote in notes on page 198.

"I was sitting at the table. We had finished dinner. We're now having dessert. And we had the most beautiful piece of chocolate cake that you've ever seen and President Xi [of China] was enjoying it....

"And we made a determination to do it, so the missiles were on the way. And I said, Mr. President, let me explain something to you. This was during dessert. "We've just fired 59 missiles, all of which hit, by the way, unbelievable, from, you know, hundreds of miles away, all of which hit, amazing."...

"It's so incredible. It's brilliant. It's genius."...

"So what happens is I said we've just launched 59 missiles heading to Iraq and I wanted you to know this. And he was eating his cake. And he was silent."

"...We're almost finished and I — what does he do, finish his dessert and go home and then they say, you know, the guy you just had dinner with just attacked a country?"

Full quote in notes on page 198.

"I have a very, very good meeting with President Xi of China. I really liked him. We had a great chemistry, I think. I mean at least I had a great chemistry — maybe he didn't like me, but I think he liked me."

"Happy Easter to everyone!"

"Things will work out fine between the U.S.A. and Russia. At the right time everyone will come to their senses & there will be lasting peace!""

Trump commented many times on Obama's infrequent golf games:

"We pay for Obama's travel so he can fundraise millions so Democrats can run on lies. Then we pay for his golf."

"Can you believe that,with all of the problems and difficulties facing the U.S., President Obama spent the day playing golf.Worse than Carter"

"Obama should play golf with Republicans & opponents rather than his small group of friends. That way maybe the terrible gridlock would end."

"Yesterday @BarackObama actually spent a full day in Washington. He didn't campaign, fund raise or play golf. Shocking."

More Trump golf comments in the notes on page 198.

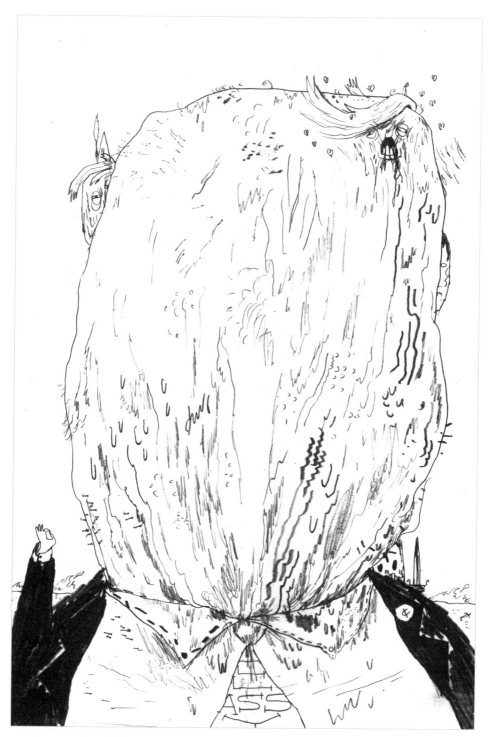

"Someone should look into who paid for the small organized rallies yesterday. The election is over!"

"No matter how much I accomplish during the ridiculous standard of the first 100 days, & it has been a lot (including S.C.), media will kill!"

TRUMP: ...He [Congressman Elijah Cummings] said you will be the greatest president. He said you will be, in front of five, six people, he said you will be the greatest president in the history of this country.

REPORTER: He disputed that slightly.

TRUMP: That's what he said. I mean, what can I tell you?

REPORTER: Yeah.

TRUMP: There's six people sitting here. What did he, what, what do you mean by slightly?

REPORTER: He said, he said that he felt like you could be a great president if and then —

TRUMP: Well he said, you'll be the greatest president in the history of, but you know what, I'll take that also...

Full quote in the note on page 198.

"...I have, seem to get very high ratings. I definitely. You know Chris Wallace had 9.2 million people, it's the highest in the history of the show. I have all the ratings for all those morning shows. When I go, they go double, triple.

"...On any, on air, [CBS "Face the Nation" host John] Dickerson had 5.2 million people. It's the highest for "Face the Nation" or as I call it, "Deface the Nation." It's the highest for "Deface the Nation" since the World Trade Center. Since the World Trade Center came down. It's a tremendous advantage."

"I have learned one thing, because I get treated very unfairly, that's what I call it, the fake media. And the fake media is not all of the media. You know they tried to say that the fake media was all the, no. The fake media is some of you. I could tell you who it is, 100 percent. Sometimes you're fake, but — but the fake media is some of the media. It bears no relationship to the truth. It's not that Fox treats me well, it's that Fox is the most accurate."

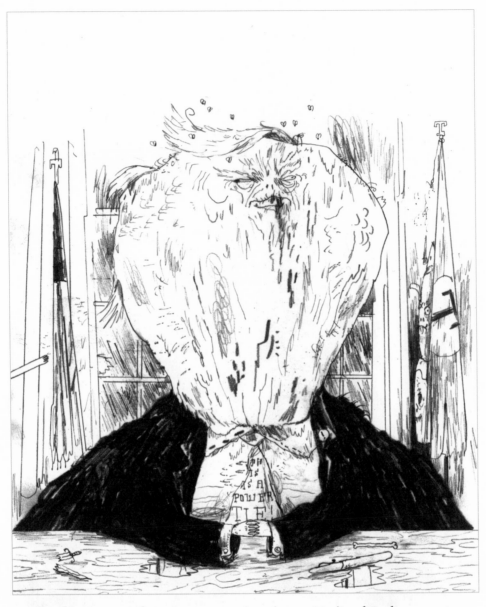

"As families prepare for summer vacations in our National Parks -
Democrats threaten to close them and shut down the government. Terrible!"

*Trump and congressional Republicans threaten to shut down the federal
government if Democrats don't agree to their demands. Bannon and Pence
lurk in the background.*

"Don't let the fake media tell you that I have changed my position on the WALL. It will get built and help stop drugs, human trafficking etc."

"First the Ninth Circuit rules against the ban & now it hits again on sanctuary cities-both ridiculous rulings. See you in the Supreme Court!"

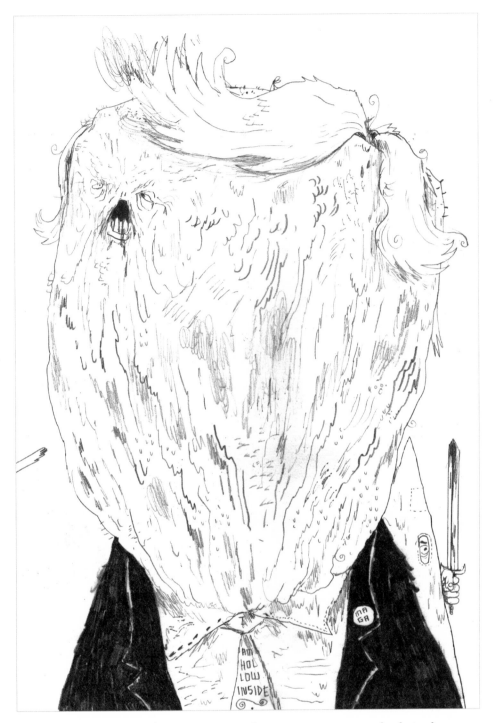

"Sanctuary cities have been very, very dangerous, very, very bad. And, you know, we've done a great job on law enforcement, we've done a great job at the border. And all of our most talented people say sanctuary cities are a disaster."

"Here, you can take that, that's the final map of the numbers," Trump said from his desk in the Oval Office, handing out maps of the United States with areas he won marked in red. "It's pretty good, right? The red is obviously us."

"Mainstream (FAKE) media refuses to state our long list of achievements, including 28 legislative signings, strong borders & great optimism!"

"Take the totally failing New York Times. Pretty soon they'll only be on the internet. The paper is getting smaller and smaller — it's starting to look like a comic book."

When reporter John Dickerson interviewed Trump and asked about "fake news" and some of the lies Trump has told, Trump abruptly ended the interview..

Full exchange between them in the note on page 199.

"Don't worry, we're going to have the wall. Don't even worry about it. ...
Rest assured. Go home, go to sleep."

The House, with Trump's support, passes the AHCA to repeal Obamacare, which will upend the health insurance market, cause millions to lose their insurance and gives a huge tax break to the wealthiest Americans.

Ryan, using a mended sword.

Trump signed an executive order preventing the IRS from expanding its restrictions on political activity by religious groups. It also provides "regulatory relief" for organizations that object on religious grounds to a provision in Obamacare that mandates employers provide certain health services, including coverage for contraception.

"We will not allow people of faith to be targeted, bullied or silenced anymore. And we will never, ever stand for religious discrimination. Never, ever."

TV evangelical leader Paula White and Vice-President Mike Pence look on.

"Rather than causing a big disruption in N.Y.C., I will be working out of my home in Bedminster, N.J. this weekend. Also saves country money!"

TRUMP: I mean, had Andrew Jackson been a little later, you wouldn't have had the Civil War. He was a very tough person, but he had a big heart, and he was really angry that he saw what was happening with regard to the Civil War. He said, "There's no reason for this." People don't realize, you know, the Civil War, you think about it, why?

REPORTER: Yeah —

TRUMP: People don't ask that question. But why was there the Civil War? Why could that one not have been worked out?

Trump's Attorney General Jefferson "Beauregard" Sessions was named after two prominent Confederates.

"Congratulations to @foxandfriends on its unbelievable ratings hike."

"The Russia-Trump collusion story is a total hoax, when will this taxpayer funded charade end?"

Trump speaking to the NRA: "You came through for me, and I am going to come through for you ... I want to thank each and every one of you, not only for your help electing true friends of the Second Amendment, but for everything you do to defend our flag and our freedom."

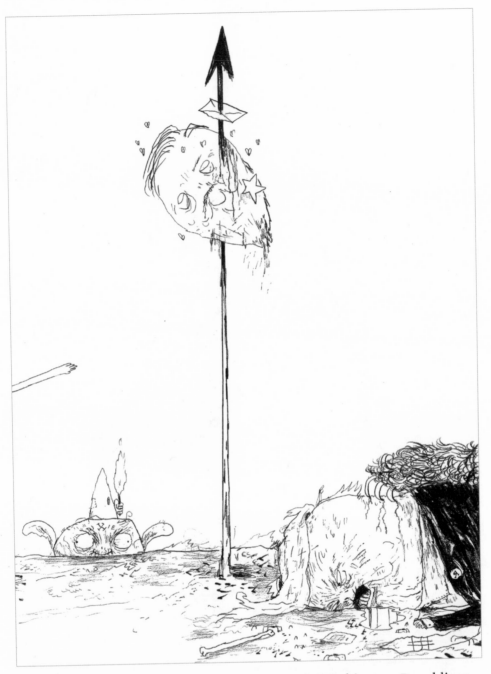

"Comey lost the confidence of almost everyone in Washington, Republican and Democrat alike. When things calm down, they will be thanking me!"

Trump fires FBI Director James Comey.

"Ask Sally Yates, under oath, if she knows how classified information got into the newspapers soon after she explained it to W.H. Counsel."

Former acting attorney general Sally Yates testified before Congress that on several occasions she warned the Trump administration about Trump's National Security Advisor pick Michael Flynn's compromised ties to Russia.

"James Comey better hope that there are no "tapes" of our conversations before he starts leaking to the press!"

Comey on the spear, Sessions under the hood and Deputy Attorney General Rod Rosenstein looking sad for his part in firing Comey.

"We have to prime the pump... Have you heard that expression used before? Because I haven't heard it. I mean, I just... I came up with it a couple of days ago."

The first recorded use of the phrase "prime the pump" was by Sir Walter Scott in 1819. It was first used in an economic sense in a Wall Street Journal article in 1933.

"Russia must be laughing up their sleeves watching as the U.S. tears itself apart over a Democrat EXCUSE for losing the election."

While meeting privately with the Russian foreign minister, Trump revealed highly classified information, jeopardizing a critical source of intelligence on the Islamic State.

"I'm not under investigation."

Trump barred the U.S. press from his meeting with the Russian foreign minister.

During his private meeting with the Russian foreign minister, Trump boasted about interfering with the Justice Department investigation of his campaign's ties to Russia.

Putin is lurking behind the Russian.

"This is the single greatest witch hunt of a politician in American history!"

Statue of Liberty and Eagle drawn from Saul Steinberg.

"With all of the illegal acts that took place in the Clinton campaign & Obama Administration, there was never a special counsel appointed!"

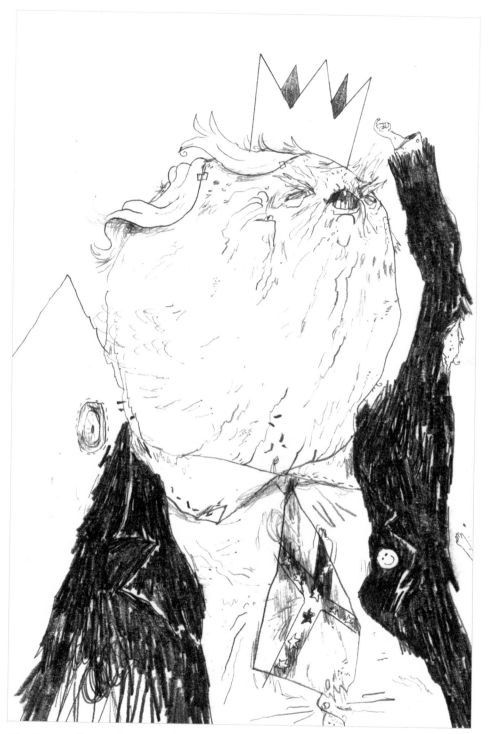

"So I can tell you that we want to bring this great country of ours together...
I hate to see anything that divides."

"Great to be in Riyadh, Saudi Arabia. Looking forward to the afternoon and evening ahead. #POTUSAbroad"

Trump receives a medal from the king of Saudi Arabia after making an arms deal: $110 billion worth of tanks, artillery, radar systems, armored personnel carriers, Blackhawk helicopters, ships, patrol boats, Patriot missiles, and THAAD missile defense systems.

The American weapons will be used in the Saudi fight against its neighbor Yemen, where more than 10,000 people have been killed over more than two years of heavy airstrikes and fighting.

"This is a battle between Good and Evil."

Trump and others at the Saudi event touch a mysterious glowing orb.

"Thank you for such a wonderful and unforgettable visit, Prime Minister @Netanyahu and @PresidentRuvi."

Trump visits the Western Wall in Jerusalem to "pray."

"Honor of a lifetime to meet His Holiness Pope Francis. I leave the Vatican more determined than ever to pursue PEACE in our world."

At a NATO meeting Trump shoved aside Dusko Markovic, the prime minister of Montenegro, as he moved to the front of a group of the leaders.

At the G7 meeting, leaders of France, Germany, Italy, Japan, Canada & UK walked the streets of Taormina, Sicily. An exhausted Trump followed in a golf cart.

"Just returned from Europe. Trip was a great success for America. Hard work but big results!"

During a normally somber Memorial Day service at Arlington National Cemetery, Trump sang along with the national anthem, at times seemingly forgetting words. Also onstage was Defense Secretary Jim Mattis.

Trump's son-in-law and close advisor Jared Kushner and Russia's ambassador to Washington discussed the possibility of setting up a secret and secure communications channel between Trump's transition team and the Kremlin using Russian diplomatic facilities.

"Despite the constant negative press covfefe,"

Trump sent a baffling text, presumably falling asleep as he typed.

Trump pulls the United States from the Paris Accords, which were meant to help curb climate change.

E.P.A. Director Scott Pruitt in the background.

"Crooked Hillary Clinton now blames everybody but herself, refuses to say she was a terrible candidate. Hits Facebook & even Dems & DNC."

"We must stop being politically correct and get down to the business of security for our people. If we don't get smart it will only get worse"

"It is my opinion that many of the leaks coming out of the White House are fabricated lies made up by the #FakeNews media. "

"Whenever you see the words 'sources say' in the fake news media, and they don't mention names.... "

"....it is very possible that those sources don't exist but are made up by fake news writers. #FakeNews is the enemy!"

"At least 7 dead and 48 wounded in terror attack and Mayor of London says there is "no reason to be alarmed!"

"Do you notice we are not having a gun debate right now? That's because they used knives and a truck!"

Trump is referring to a terror attack in the U.K.

"People, the lawyers and the courts can call it whatever they want, but I am calling it what we need and what it is, a TRAVEL BAN!"

"The Justice Dept. should have stayed with the original Travel Ban, not the watered down, politically correct version they submitted to S.C."

"The Justice Dept. should ask for an expedited hearing of the watered down Travel Ban before the Supreme Court - & seek much tougher version!"

"In any event we are EXTREME VETTING people coming into the U.S. in order to help keep our country safe. The courts are slow and political!"

"I need loyalty, I expect loyalty."

Former F.B.I. Director James Comey reported Trump saying this to him in an attempt to get Comey to stop the investigation into then-National Security Council Chair Michael Flynn. Trump's son-in-law Jared Kushner, in the center bottom of the drawing, was involved in the Russian connections.

"Despite so many false statements and lies, total and complete vindication... and WOW, Comey is a leaker!"

"Congratulations to Jeb Hensarling & Republicans on successful House vote to repeal major parts of the 2010 Dodd-Frank financial law. GROWTH!"

"Never has there been a president, with few exceptions ... who has passed more legislation, done more things..."

With TV cameras rolling, Trump had cabinet members one by one declare how wonderful and awesome he is.

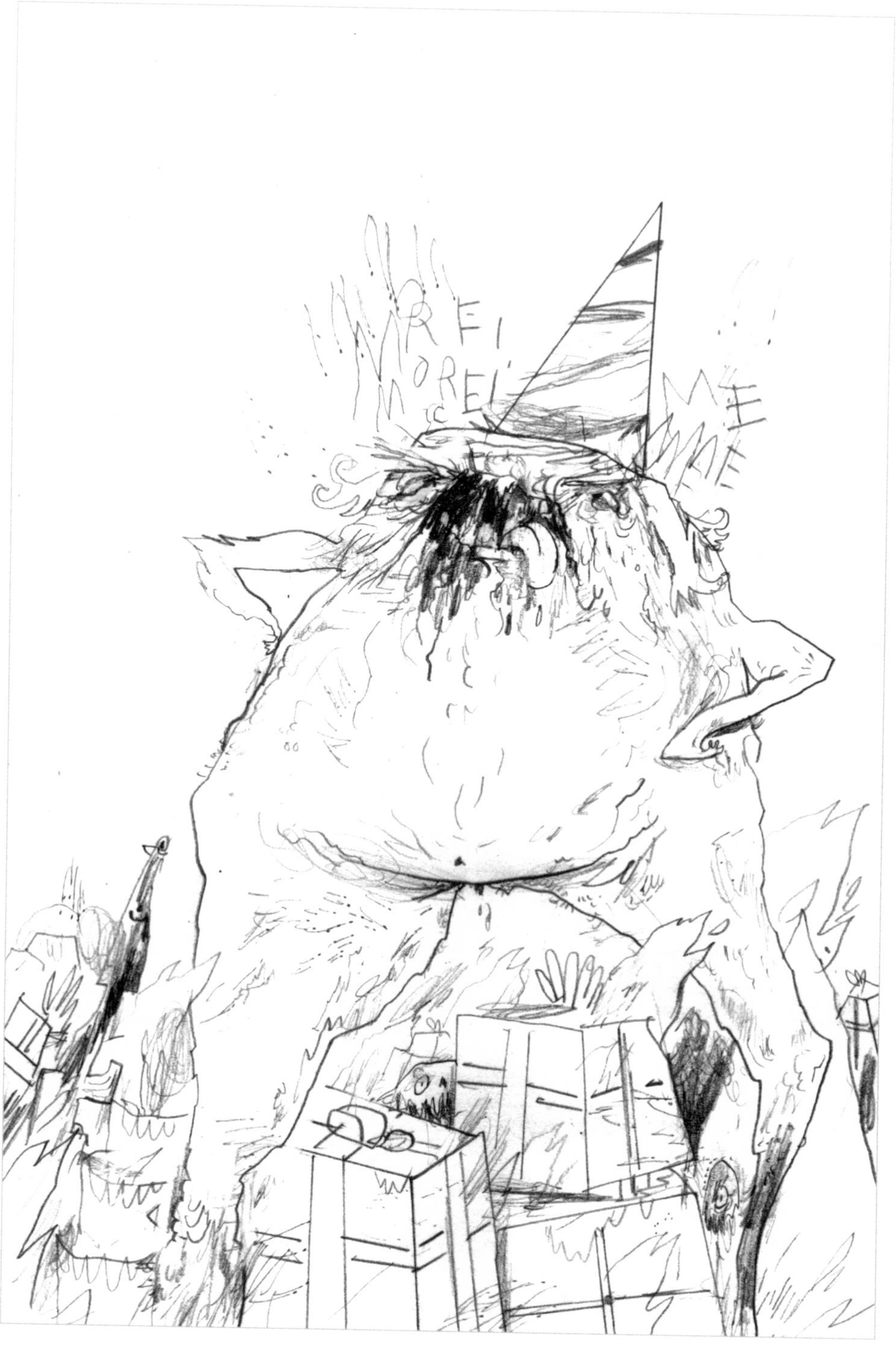

Trump turned 71 years old.

"They made up a phony collusion with the Russians story, found zero proof, so now they go for obstruction of justice on the phony story. Nice"

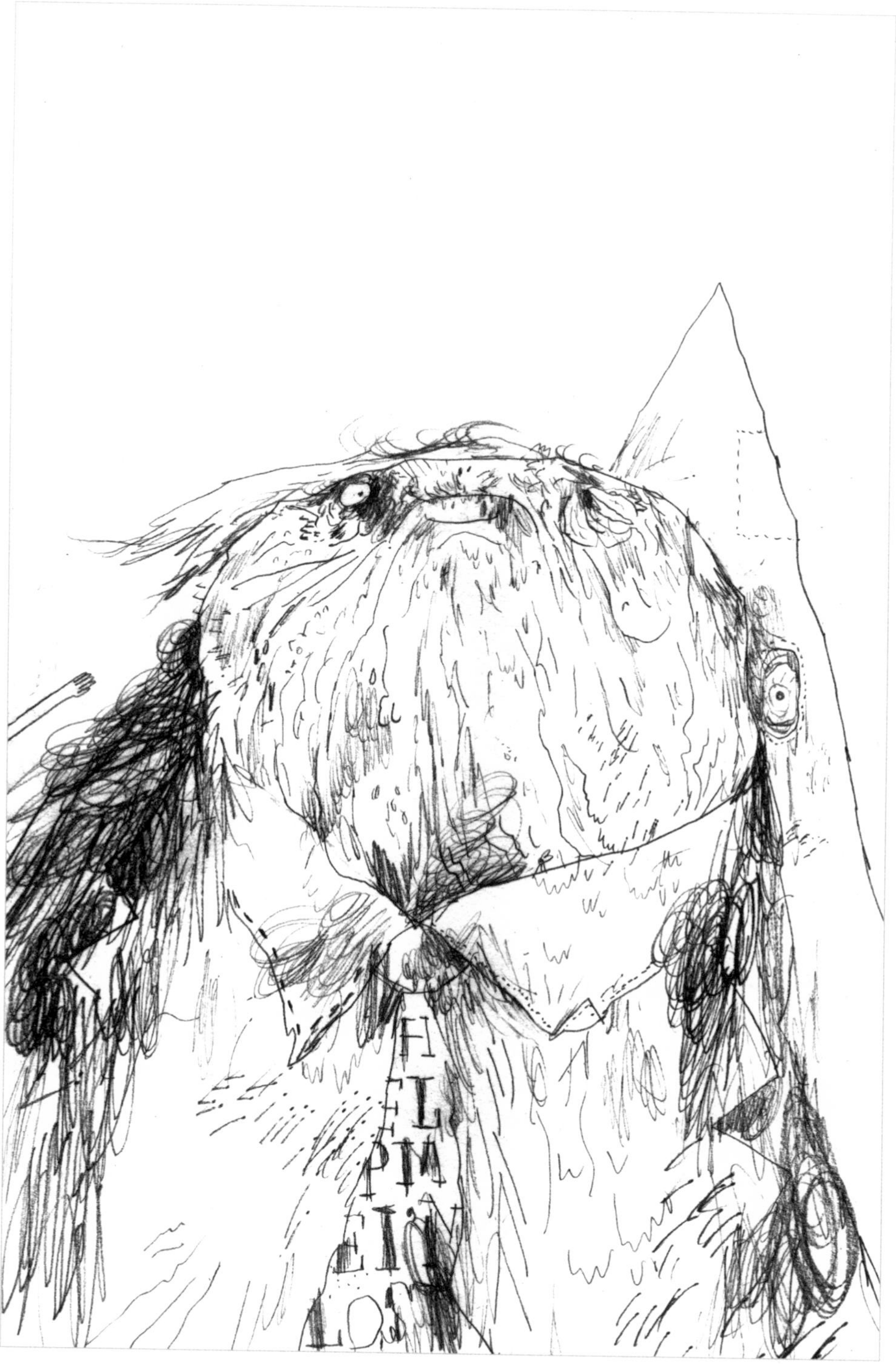

“The Fake News Media hates when I use what has turned out to be my very powerful Social Media - over 100 million people! I can go around them”

"You are witnessing the single greatest WITCH HUNT in American political history - led by some very bad and conflicted people! #MAGA"

"Camp David is a very special place. An honor to have spent the weekend there. Military runs it so well and are so proud of what they do!"

"We're going to have insurance for everybody"

"I was the first & only potential GOP candidate to state there will be no cuts to Social Security, Medicare & Medicaid"

"We are not going to let the same failed and tired voices in Washington keep us from delivering the change you voted for and the change that you deserve."

"People are saying, where's the healthcare? Where's the healthcare? Well, I've done in five months what other people haven't done in years."

"You know, healthcare is a very difficult situation... It's a very complicated situation from the standpoint, you do something that's good for one group but bad for another. It's a very, very narrow path."

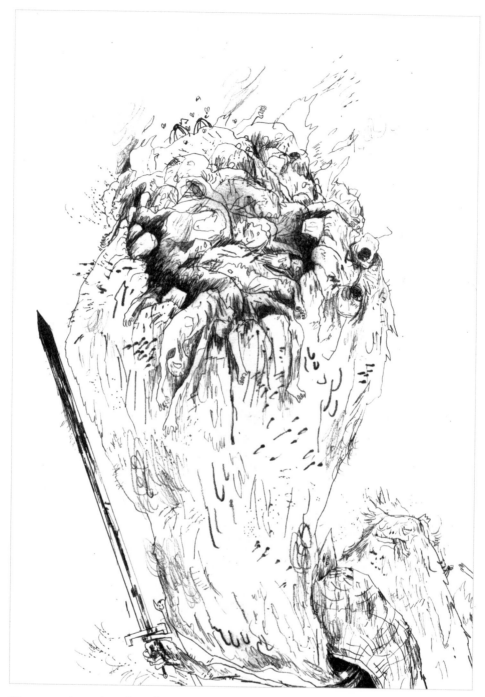

"I cannot imagine that these very fine Republican Senators would allow the American people to suffer a broken ObamaCare any longer!"

Senate Majority Leader Mitch McConnell

"Republican Senators are working very hard to get there, with no help from the Democrats. Not easy! Perhaps just let OCare crash & burn!"

"The Democrats have become nothing but OBSTRUCTIONISTS, they have no policies or ideas. All they do is delay and complain. They own ObamaCare!"

"I just finished a great meeting with the Republican Senators concerning HealthCare. They really want to get it right, unlike OCare!"

Several Trump-owned golf clubs have been displaying fake Time magazine covers featuring Trump's photo.

"I heard poorly rated @Morning_Joe speaks badly of me (don't watch anymore). Then how come low I.Q. Crazy Mika, along with Psycho Joe, came.."

"...to Mar-a-Lago 3 nights in a row around New Year's Eve, and insisted on joining me. She was bleeding badly from a face-lift. I said no!"

Trump feuds with some television news hosts.

"Watched low rated @Morning_Joe for first time in long time. FAKE NEWS. He called me to stop a National Enquirer article. I said no! Bad show"

"Crazy Joe Scarborough and dumb as a rock Mika are not bad people, but their low rated show is dominated by their NBC bosses. Too bad!"

"Numerous states are refusing to give information to the very distinguished VOTER FRAUD PANEL. What are they trying to hide?"

Kansas Secretary of State Kris Kobach is leading the effort to disenfranchise millions of Americans.

Trump retweeted a video clip showing him in a wrestling match body-slamming a CNN logo-headed person and then walking away with a smug grin on his face.

"Spoke yesterday with the King of Saudi Arabia about peace in the Middle-East. Interesting things are happening!"

The dishonest media will NEVER keep us from accomplishing our objectives on behalf of our GREAT AMERICAN PEOPLE! #AmericaFirst

Drawing based on a painting by Goya.

In his first few months heading the EPA, Administrator Scott Pruitt has moved to undo, delay or otherwise block more than 30 environmental rules.

"My use of social media is not Presidential - it's MODERN DAY PRESIDENTIAL. Make America Great Again!"

"I strongly pressed President Putin twice about Russian meddling in our election. He vehemently denied it. I've already given my opinion....."

"When I left Conference Room for short meetings with Japan and other countries, I asked Ivanka to hold seat. Very standard. Angela M agrees!"

"If Chelsea Clinton were asked to hold the seat for her mother, as her mother gave our country away, the Fake News would say CHELSEA FOR PRES!"

"I will represent our country well and fight for its interests! Fake News Media will never cover me accurately but who cares! We will #MAGA!"

"THE WEST WILL NEVER BE BROKEN. Our values will PREVAIL. Our people will THRIVE and our civilization will TRIUMPH!"

"My son is a high-quality person and I applaud his transparency."

Donald Trump, Jr. is questioned about his meetings with Russian agents during the presidential campaign.

"My son is a wonderful young man... Don is, as many of you know, Don, he's a good boy. He's a good kid."

".@WashTimes states "Democrats have willfully used Moscow disinformation to influence the presidential election against Donald Trump."

Kellyanne Conway on TV.

"You didn't let me down and I will never, ever let you down, you know that."

Trump prayed with evangelical leaders in the Oval Office

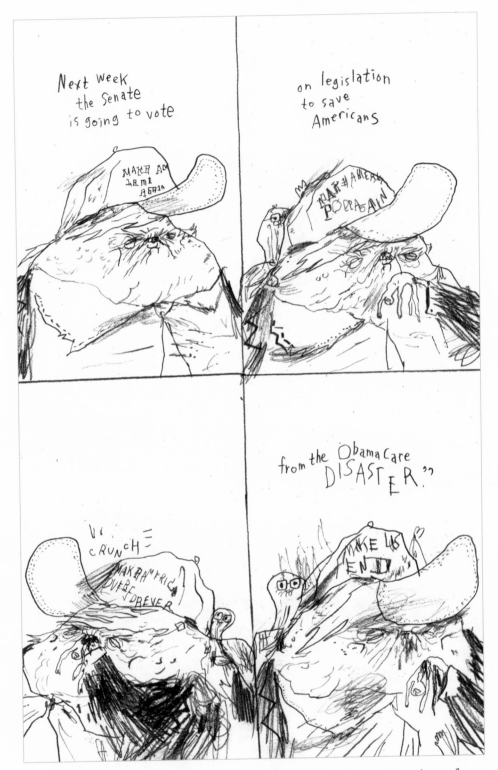

"Next week the Senate is going to vote on legislation to save Americans from the ObamaCare DISASTER. #WeeklyAddress"

"MAKE AMERICA GREAT AGAIN!"

"Republicans should just REPEAL failing ObamaCare now & work on a new Healthcare Plan that will start from a clean slate. Dems will join in!"

"The Republicans never discuss how good their healthcare bill is, & it will get even better at lunchtime.The Dems scream death as OCare dies!"

"So Jeff Sessions takes the job, gets into the job, recuses himself. I then have — which, frankly, I think is very unfair to the president. How do you take a job and then recuse yourself? ... It's extremely unfair, and that's a mild word, to the president."

"My son Donald openly gave his e-mails to the media & authorities whereas Crooked Hillary Clinton deleted (& acid washed) her 33,000 e-mails!"

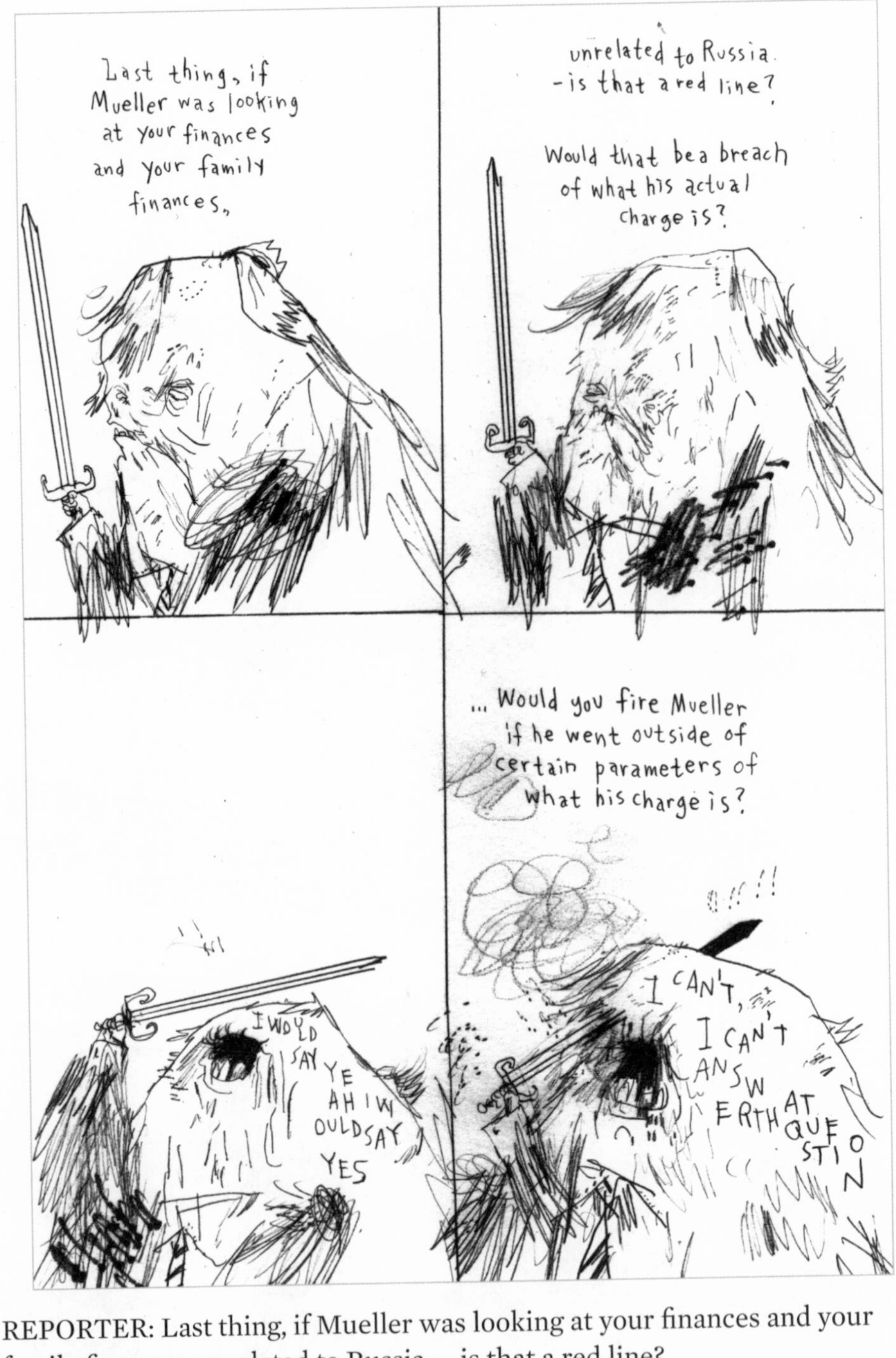
Last thing, if Mueller was looking at your finances and your family finances,
unrelated to Russia. -is that a red line?
Would that be a breach of what his actual charge is?
I WOULD SAY YE AH I W OULDSAY YES
... Would you fire Mueller if he went outside of certain parameters of what his charge is?
I CAN'T, I CAN'T ANSW ERTHAT QUE STION

REPORTER: Last thing, if Mueller was looking at your finances and your family finances, unrelated to Russia — is that a red line?
REPORTER: Would that be a breach of what his actual charge is?
TRUMP: I would say yeah. I would say yes.
...
REPORTER: Would you fire Mueller if he went outside of certain parameters of what his charge is?
TRUMP: I can't, I can't answer that question because I don't think it's going to happen.

SOURCES AND NOTES

Pg 7 *(01/20/17)* https://www.npr.org/2017/01/20/510629447/watch-live-president-trumps-inauguration-ceremony

Pg 8 *(01/21/17)* https://twitter.com/realDonaldTrump/status/823150055418920960

Pg 9 *(01/22/17)* https://www.cnn.com/2017/01/22/politics/kellyanne-conway-alternative-facts/

Pg 10 *(01/23/17)* http://abcnews.go.com/Politics/week-transcript-22-17-kellyanne-conway-sen-john/story?id=44954948

Pg 11 *(01/24/17)* https://www.lawfareblog.com/president-trump-speaks-cia-headquarters More complete statement: ""So I only like to say that because I love honesty. I like honest reporting. I will tell you the final time: although I will say it, when you let in your thousands of other people that had been trying to come in, because I am coming back.We may have to get you a larger room. [laughter, applause] We may have to get you a larger room.
"And maybe - maybe - it'll be built by somebody that knows how to build and we won't have columns [laughter] You understand that? We'd get rid of the columns.
"I just wanted to really say that I love you. I respect you. There's nobody that I respect more. You're going to do a fantastic job. And we're going to start winning again. And you're going to be leading the charge.
"So thank you all very much. Thank you, beautiful. Thank you all very much.
"Have a good day.
"I'll be back. I'll be back. Thank you."

Pg 12 *(01/25/17)* https://www.lawfareblog.com/president-trump-speaks-cia-headquarters

Pg 13 *(01/26/17)* http://abcnews.go.com/Politics/transcript-abc-news-anchor-david-muir-interviews-president/story?id=45047602

Pg 14 *(01/27/17)* https://www.npr.org/sections/thetwo-way/2017/01/26/511903885/trump-s-refugee-plan-will-prioritize-christian-refugees

Pg 15 *(01/28/17)* https://www.nytimes.com/2017/01/26/business/media/stephen-bannon-trump-news-media.html?_r=0

Pg 16 *(01/29/17)* http://www.bbc.com/news/world-us-canada-38695593

Pg 17 *(01/30/17)* http://abcnews.go.com/Politics/transcript-abc-news-anchor-david-muir-interviews-president/story?id=45047602

Pg 18 *(01/31/17)* http://www.jpost.com/American-Politics/Trump-offers-strategist-Bannon-permanent-seat-on-National-Security-Council-479966

Pg 19 *(02/01/17)* http://www.slate.com/blogs/the_slatest/2017/01/30/steve_bannon_and_stephen_miller_s_muslim_ban_is_about_white_nationalism.html

Pg 20 *(02/02/17)* https://www.nytimes.com/2017/01/31/us/politics/supreme-court-nominee-trump.html

Pg 21 *(02/03/17)* http://www.latimes.com/nation/nationnow/la-na-pol-trump-mexico-call-20170201-story.html

Pg 22 *(02/04/17)* http://thehill.com/policy/finance/317756-trump-says-business-friends-cant-get-loans-because-of-dodd-frank

Pg 23 *(02/05/17)* https://twitter.com/realDonaldTrump/status/827867311054974976

Pg 24 *(02/06/17)* https://www.sbnation.com/2017/2/5/14516156/donald-trump-interview-transcript-bill-oreilly-super-bowl-2017

Pg 25 *(02/07/17)* https://twitter.com/realDonaldTrump/status/828575949268606977

Pg 26 *(02/08/17)* https://www.americanprogress.org/issues/education-postsecondary/news/2017/01/12/296231/conflicts-of-devos/ Full list:
Senators who voted to confirm Devos with the amounts her family has given them since 1980:
Sen. Roy Blunt (R-MO) - $33,100
Sen. Richard Burr (R-NC) - $43,200
Sen. Bill Cassidy (R-LA) - $70,200
Sen. Tom Cotton (R-AR) - $26,000
Sen. Steve Daines (R-MT) - $46,800
Sen. Cory Gardner (R-CO) - $49,800
Sen. Chuck Grassley (R-IA) - $21,600
Sen. Ron Johnson (R-WI) - $48,600
Sen. John McCain (R-AZ) - $50,600
Sen. Mitch McConnell (R-KY) - $36,400
Sen. David Perdue (R-GA) - $23,400
Sen. Rob Portman (R-OH) - $51,000
Sen. Mike Rounds (R-SD) - $46,800
Sen. Marco Rubio (R-FL) - $98,300
Sen. Timothy E. Scott (R-SC) - $49,200
Sen. Dan Sullivan (R-AK) - $23,400
Sen. John Thune (R-SD) - $17,550
Sen. Thom Tillis (R-NC) - $70,200
Sen. Pat Toomey (R-PA) - $60,050
Sen. Todd Young (R-IN) - $48,600
Total: $957,950

Pg 27 *(02/09/17)* https://www.thedailybeast.com/jeff-sessions-wanted-to-drop-the-case-against-kkk-lynching-attorney-testified and https://www.nytimes.com/interactive/2017/01/08/us/politics/jeff-sessions-on-the-issues.html?_r=0 and http://edition.cnn.com/TRANSCRIPTS/1701/10/cg.01.html

Pg 28 *(02/10/17)* https://twitter.com/realDonaldTrump/status/829836231802515457

Pg 29 *(02/11/17)* https://www.washingtonpost.com/world/national-security/national-security-adviser-flynn-discussed-sanctions-with-russian-ambassador-despite-denials-officials-say/2017/02/09/f85b29d6-ee11-11e6-b4ff-ac2cf509efe5_story.html?utm_term=.001c426bf717

Pg 30 *(02/12/17)* https://www.nytimes.com/2017/02/05/us/politics/trump-white-house-aides-strategy.html

Pg 31 *(02/13/17)* https://abcnews.go.com/Politics/week-transcript-12-17-stephen-miller-bob-ferguson/story?id=45426805

Pg 32 *(02/14/17)* https://www.nytimes.com/2017/02/13/us/politics/donald-trump-national-security-adviser-michael-flynn.html

Pg 33 *(02/15/17)* xxxxxx and https://twitter.com/realDonaldTrump/status/830804130692268032

Pg 34 *(02/16/17)* https://www.independent.co.uk/news/world/americas/us-politics/donald-trump-russia-leaks-fake-news-claims-quote-a7584516.html More from that press conference:
Reporter: "You said today that you had the biggest electoral margin since Ronald Reagan, with 304, 306 electoral votes. In fact, president Obama got 365. President Obama 332, and George H.W. Bush 426, when he won as president. So why should should Americans trust...
Trump: "I was given that information, I don't know. I was just given that information. It was a very, very big margin.".
Reporter: "I guess my question is, why should Americans trust you when you accuse the information they receive of being fake when you're providing information that..."
Trump: "Well I don't know, I was given that information. Actually I've seen that information around. But it was a very substantial victory, do you agree with that?"

Pg 35 *(02/17/17)* https://twitter.com/realDonaldTrump/status/831830548565852160 and https://twitter.com/realDonaldTrump/status/831837514226921472 and https://twitter.com/realDonaldTrump/status/831840306161123328

Pg 36 *(02/18/17)* https://twitter.com/realDonaldTrump/status/827655062835052544

Pg 37 *(02/19/17)* https://www.cosmopolitan.com/politics/a8946052/donald-trump-mar-a-lago-trips-10-million-taxpayers/

Pg 38 *(02/20/17)* http://www.chicagotribune.com/news/nationworld/politics/ct-trump-lifestyle-taxpayers-20170216-story.html and http://money.cnn.com/2017/02/17/news/dubai-golf-club-trump/

Pg 39 *(02/21/17)* https://talkingpointsmemo.com/edblog/a-big-shoe-just-dropped

Pg 40 *(02/22/17)* https://www.politico.com/story/2017/01/full-text-trump-pence-remarks-cia-headquarters-233978

Pg 41 *(02/23/17)* https://www.washingtonpost.com/local/education/trump-administration-rolls-back-protections-for-transgender-students/2017/02/22/550a83b4-f913-11e6-bf01-d47f8cf9b643_story.html?noredirect=on&utm_term=.9d1967120243

Pg 42 *(02/24/17)* https://www.politico.com/story/2017/02/trump-tweet-media-enemy-american-people-235150

Pg 43 *(02/25/17)* https://www.washingtonpost.com/world/national-security/sessions-spoke-twice-with-russian-ambassador-during-trumps-presidential-campaign-justice-officials-say/2017/03/01/77205eda-feac-11e6-99b4-9e613af-eb09f_story.html?noredirect=on&utm_term=.e23815300f0e

Pg 44 *(02/26/17)* https://twitter.com/realDonaldTrump/status/835608648625836032

Pg 45 *(02/27/17)* https://twitter.com/realDonaldTrump/status/838441522546769923

Pg 46 *(02/28/17)* https://www.nytimes.com/2017/02/25/us/ice-immigrant-deportations-trump.html

Pg 50 *(03/01/17)* https://twitter.com/realDonaldTrump/status/837989835818287106

Pg 51 *(03/02/17)* https://www.romper.com/p/this-list-of-bills-introduced-under-trump-is-more-important-than-any-of-his-tweets-42533
A partial list of bills introduced: 1. HR 861 Terminate the Environmental Protection Agency
2. HR 610 Vouchers for Public Education
3. HR 899 Terminate the Department of Education
4. HJR 69 Repeal Rule Protecting Wildlife
5. HR 370 Repeal Affordable Care Act
6. HR 354 Defund Planned Parenthood
7. HR 785 National Right to Work (this one ends unions)
8. HR 83 Mobilizing Against Sanctuary Cities Bill
9. HR 147 Criminalizing Abortion ("Prenatal Nondiscrimination Act")

Pg 52 *(03/03/17)* https://www.nytimes.com/2017/02/16/us/politics/affordable-care-act-congress.html

Pg 53 *(03/04/17)* https://www.nbcnews.com/politics/white-house/president-trump-signs-new-immigration-executive-order-n724276

Pg 54 *(03/05/17)* https://twitter.com/
realDonaldTrump/status/839433951957696513
and https://twitter.com/realDonaldTrump/
status/839433678275153921

Pg 55 *(03/06/17)* https://twitter.com/
realDonaldTrump/status/839883804315684864

Pg 56 *(03/07/17)* https://www.politico.com/
story/2017/03/trump-monthly-jobs-numbers-
sean-spicer-235936

Pg 57 *(03/08/17)* https://twitter.com/
realDonaldTrump/status/841966077005463553

Pg 58 *(03/09/17)* https://www.nytimes.
com/2017/03/07/us/politics/affordable-care-act-
obama-care-health.html?_r=1

Pg 59 *(03/10/17)* https://www.tennessean.com/
story/news/politics/2017/03/15/trump-rally-
nashville/99159270/

Pg 60 *(03/11/17)* https://thinkprogress.org/
trump-mar-a-lago-trump-branded-properties-
weekends-41d373bbe97a/#.yfknqa41b

Pg 61 *(03/12/17)* http://nymag.com/daily/
intelligencer/2017/03/white-house-says-cutting-
meals-on-wheels-is-compassionate.html

Pg 62 *(03/13/17)* http://time.com/4703622/
president-trump-speech-transcript-travel-ban-
ruling/

Pg 63 *(03/14/17)* https://talkingpointsmemo.
com/edblog/the-real-story--4

Pg 64 *(03/15/17)* https://www.nytimes.
com/2017/03/21/us/politics/neil-gorsuch-
confirmation-hearings.html

Pg 65 *(03/16/17)* https://www.cbo.gov/sites/
default/files/115th-congress-2017-2018/
costestimate/americanhealthcareact.pdf

Pg 66 *(03/17/17)* https://www.nytimes.
com/2017/03/24/us/politics/health-care-
affordable-care-act.html

Pg 67 *(03/18/17)* https://www.independent.
co.uk/news/world/americas/us-politics/donald-
trump-react-healthcare-bill-vote-pull-congress-
obamacare-democrats-a7649236.html

Pg 68 *(03/19/17)* http://time.com/4710456/
donald-trump-time-interview-truth-falsehood/

Pg 69 *(03/20/17)* https://www.cnn.
com/2017/03/23/politics/trump-time-interview-
wiretaps-falsehoods/

Pg 70 *(03/21/17)* https://twitter.com/
realDonaldTrump/status/847061031293779969

Pg 71 *(03/22/17)* http://time.com/4710456/

donald-trump-time-interview-truth-falsehood/

Pg 72 *(03/23/17)* https://www.cnn.
com/2017/03/27/politics/ivanka-trump-jared-
kushner-white-house-influence/

Pg 73 *(03/24/17)* https://forward.com/news/
longform/366181/exclusive-nazi-allied-group-
claims-top-trump-aide-sebastian-gorka-as-
sworn/ and https://talkingpointsmemo.com/
dc/sebastian-gorka-horthy-medal-father-anti-
communist

Pg 74 *(03/25/17)* https://www.politico.com/
story/2017/03/mike-pence-johnny-isakson-
planned-parenthood-vote-senate-236702

Pg 75 *(03/26/17)* https://twitter.com/
realDonaldTrump/status/848153860602507264

Pg 76 *(03/27/17)* https://twitter.com/
realDonaldTrump/status/848519587675201538

Pg 77 *(03/28/17)* https://metro.
co.uk/2017/04/07/trump-tweet-about-world-
war-iii-comes-back-to-haunt-him-6560159/

Pg 78 *(03/29/17)* https://www.nytimes.
com/2017/04/05/us/politics/donald-trump-
interview-new-york-times-transcript.html

Pg 79 *(03/30/17)* https://twitter.com/
realDonaldTrump/status/829384587482656768

Pg 80 *(04/01/17)* https://www.nytimes.
com/2017/04/05/us/politics/donald-trump-
interview-new-york-times-transcript.html

Pg 81 *(04/01/17)* https://www.nytimes.
com/2017/04/12/world/middleeast/trump-syria-
russia.html?_r=0

Pg 82 *(04/02/17)* https://twitter.com/
realDonaldTrump/status/852297935219982336

Pg 83 *(04/03/17)* https://twitter.com/
realDonaldTrump/status/852318522139168769

Pg 84 *(04/04/17)* https://twitter.com/
realDonaldTrump/status/851767718248361986

Pg 85 *(04/05/17)* https://www.whitehouse.gov/
briefings-statements/remarks-president-trump-
2017-north-americas-building-trades-unions-
national-legislative-conference/

Pg 86 *(04/06/17)* https://www.whitehouse.gov/
briefings-statements/remarks-president-trump-
press-aboard-air-force-one-en-route-west-palm-
beach-florida/

Pg 87 *(04/07/17)* https://www.cnn.
com/2017/04/07/politics/neil-gorsuch-senate-
vote/index.html

Pg 88 *(04/08/17)* https://www.cnn.
com/2017/04/06/politics/donald-trump-syria-

military/index.html

Pg 89 *(04/09/17)* http://thehill.com/homenews/administration/328024-trump-spotted-at-florida-golf-club

Pg 90 *(04/10/17)* https://www.whitehouse.gov/briefings-statements/remarks-president-trump-justice-gorsuch-swearing-justice-gorsuch-supreme-court/

Pg 91 *(04/11/17)* https://www.politico.com/blogs/donald-trump-administration/2017/04/trump-schedule-today-white-house-237069

Pg 92 *(04/12/17)* https://www.washingtonpost.com/news/the-fix/wp/2017/04/12/president-trumps-throughly-confusing-fox-business-interview-annotated/?utm_term=.fcdadcda37d0

Pg 93-95 *(04/13/17-04/15/17)* https://www.washingtonpost.com/news/the-fix/wp/2017/04/12/president-trumps-throughly-confusing-fox-business-interview-annotated* Full quote:
"I was sitting at the table. We had finished dinner. We're now having dessert. And we had the most beautiful piece of chocolate cake that you've ever seen and President Xi [of China] was enjoying it.

"And I was given the message from the generals that the ships are locked and loaded, what do you do?

"And we made a determination to do it, so the missiles were on the way. And I said, Mr. President, let me explain something to you. This was during dessert.

"We've just fired 59 missiles, all of which hit, by the way, unbelievable, from, you know, hundreds of miles away, all of which hit, amazing."
BARTIROMO: "Unmanned? Brilliant".
TRUMP: "It's so incredible. It's brilliant. It's genius."
...
"So what happens is I said we've just launched 59 missiles heading to Iraq and I wanted you to know this. And he was eating his cake. And he was silent."
BARTIROMO: "(INAUDIBLE) to Syria?"
TRUMP: "Yes. Heading toward Syria. In other words, we've just launched 59 missiles heading toward Syria. And I want you to know that, because I didn't want him to go home. We were almost finished. It was a full day in Palm Beach. We're almost finished and I — what does he do, finish his dessert and go home and then they say, you know, the guy you just had dinner with just attacked a country?"

Pg 96 *(04/16/17)* https://twitter.com/realDonaldTrump/status/853584968047636480

Pg 97 *(04/17/17)* https://twitter.com/realDonaldTrump/status/852510810287075329

Pg 98 *(04/18/17)* https://www.sbnation.com/golf/2017/3/27/15073086/donald-trump-tweets-barack-obama-golf
More comments: "While our wonderful president [Obama] was out playing golf all day, the TSA is falling apart, just like our government! Airports a total disaster!"
"Obama has admitted that he spends his mornings watching @ESPN. Then he plays golf, fundraises & grants amnesty to illegals."
"If Obama resigns from office NOW, thereby doing a great service to the country—I will give him free lifetime golf at any one of my courses!"
"President Obama played golf yesterday???"
"Obama should play golf with Republicans & opponents rather than his small group of friends. That way maybe the terrible gridlock would end."
"I play golf to relax. My company is in great shape. @BarackObama plays golf to escape work while America goes down the drain."

Pg 99 *(04/19/17)* https://twitter.com/realDonaldTrump/status/853597199619543041

Pg 100 *(04/20/17)* https://twitter.com/realDonaldTrump/status/855373184861962240

Pg 101 *(04/21/17)* https://apnews.com/c810d7de280a47e88848b0ac74690c83*
TRUMP: I think (I) can to an extent. But there's a, there's a basic hard-line core that you can't break though, OK, that you can't break through. There's a hard-line group you can't break through, you can't. It's sad. You can't. Look, I met with Congressman Cummings and I really liked him, a lot. Elijah Cummings (of Maryland). I really liked him a lot. And during the conversation because we have a very strong mutual feeling on drug prices. He came to see me, at my invitation, because I saw him talking about, he came to see me about drug prices because drug prices are ridiculous. And I am going to get them way, way, way down and he liked that. He said you will be the greatest president. He said you will be, in front of five, six people, he said you will be the greatest president in the history of this country.
AP: He disputed that slightly.
TRUMP: That's what he said. I mean, what can I tell you?
AP: Yeah.
TRUMP: There's six people sitting here. What did he, what, what do you mean by slightly?
AP: He said, he said that he felt like you could be a great president if and then —
TRUMP: Well he said, you'll be the greatest president in the history of, but you know what, I'll take that also, but that you could be. But he said, will be the greatest president but I would also accept the other. In other words, if you do your job, but I accept that. Then I watched him interviewed and it was like he never even was here. It's incredible. I watched him interviewed a week later and it's like he was never in my office. And you can even say that.

Pg 102 *(04/22/17)* https://apnews.com/c810d7de280a47e88848b0ac74690c83

Pg 103 (04/23/17) https://apnews.com/
c810d7de280a47e88848b0ac74690c83

Pg 104 (04/24/17) https://twitter.com/
realDonaldTrump/status/857605104417026049

Pg 105 (04/25/17) https://twitter.com/
realDonaldTrump/status/856849388026687492

Pg 106 (04/26/17) https://twitter.com/
realDonaldTrump/status/857177434210304001

Pg 107 (04/27/17) https://www.
washingtonexaminer.com/exclusive-interview-
trump-absolutely-looking-at-breaking-up-9th-
circuit

Pg 108 (04/28/17) https://www.reuters.com/
article/us-usa-trump-100days-idUSKBN17U0CA

Pg 109 (04/29/17) https://twitter.com/
realDonaldTrump/status/858375278686613504

Pg 110 (04/30/17) https://www.nbcnews.com/
storyline/president-trumps-first-100-days/
trump-touts-first-100-days-record-slams-press-
campaign-style-n752916

Pg 111 (05/01/17) https://www.cbsnews.com/
news/president-trump-oval-office-interview-
cbs-this-morning-full-transcript/ Full transcript:
JOHN DICKERSON: Did President Obama give
you any advice that was helpful? That you think,
wow, he really was–
 DONALD TRUMP: – Well, he was very nice to
me. But after that, we've had some difficulties.
So it doesn't matter. You know, words are less
important to me than deeds. And you– you saw
what happened with surveillance. And everybody
saw what happened with surveillance–
JOHN DICKERSON: Difficulties how?
PRESIDENT DONALD TRUMP: – and I thought
that – well, you saw what happened with
surveillance. And I think that was inappropriate,
but that's the way–
JOHN DICKERSON: What does that mean, sir?
PRESIDENT DONALD TRUMP: You can figure
that out yourself.
JOHN DICKERSON: Well, I– the reason I ask is
you said he was– you called him "sick and bad".
PRESIDENT DONALD TRUMP: Look, you can
figure it out yourself. He was very nice to me with
words, but– and when I was with him – but after
that, there has been no relationship.
JOHN DICKERSON: But you stand by that claim
about him?
PRESIDENT DONALD TRUMP: I don't stand by
anything. I just– you can take it the way you want.
I think our side's been proven very strongly. And
everybody's talking about it. And frankly it should
be discussed. I think that is a very big surveillance
of our citizens. I think it's a very big topic. And
it's a topic that should be number one. And we
should find out what the hell is going on.
JOHN DICKERSON: I just wanted to find out,
though. You're– you're the president of the

United States. You said he was "sick and bad"
because he had tapped you– I'm just–
PRESIDENT DONALD TRUMP: You can take–
any way. You can take it any way you want.
JOHN DICKERSON: But I'm asking you. Because
you don't want it to be–
PRESIDENT DONALD TRUMP: You don't–
JOHN DICKERSON: –fake news. I want to hear
it from–
PRESIDENT DONALD TRUMP: You don't have
to–
JOHN DICKERSON: –President Trump.
PRESIDENT DONALD TRUMP: –ask me. You
don't have to ask me.
JOHN DICKERSON: Why not?
PRESIDENT DONALD TRUMP: Because I
have my own opinions. You can have your own
opinions.
JOHN DICKERSON: But I want to know your
opinions. You're the president of the United
States.
PRESIDENT DONALD TRUMP: Okay, it's
enough. Thank you. Thank you very much.

Pg 112 (05/02/17) https://www.
washingtonpost.com/politics/100-days-
in-trump-invigorates-enchants-crowd-
during-rally-in-harrisburg-pa/2017/04/29/
c656d764-2aa7-11e7-a616-d7c8a68c1a66_story.
html?utm_term=.80884753a803

Pg 113 (05/03/17) https://www.theguardian.com/
us-news/2017/may/04/republican-healthcare-
bill-passes-house-vote-obamacare-repeal

Pg 114 (05/04/17) https://www.cnn.
com/2017/05/03/politics/trump-religious-
liberty-executive-order/

Pg 115 (05/05/17) https://twitter.com/
realDonaldTrump/status/860479885566980096

Pg 116 (05/06/17) http://thehill.com/homenews/
administration/331349-trump-why-was-there-
the-civil-war

Pg 117 (05/07/17) https://twitter.com/
realDonaldTrump/status/860088511202029569

Pg 118 (05/08/17) https://twitter.com/
realDonaldTrump/status/861713823505494016

Pg 119 (05/09/17) https://www.theguardian.com/
us-news/2018/jan/30/going-low-a-year-of-top-
trump-quotes-to-rival-the-white-houses-list

Pg 120 (05/10/17) https://twitter.com/
realDonaldTrump/status/862267781336752128

Pg 121 (05/11/17) https://twitter.com/
realDonaldTrump/status/861592420043157504
and https://www.nytimes.com/2017/05/08/
us/politics/michael-flynn-sally-yates-hearing.
html?_r=0

Pg 122 (05/12/17) https://twitter.com/
realDonaldTrump/status/863007411132649473

Pg 123 *(05/13/17)* https://www.nationalreview.com/corner/trump-claims-he-coined-prime-pump/

Pg 124 *(05/14/17)* https://twitter.com/realDonaldTrump/status/862767872879325185

Pg 125-126 *(05/15/17 - 05/16/17)* https://www.nytimes.com/2017/05/19/us/politics/trump-russia-comey.html?

Pg 127 *(05/17/17)* https://twitter.com/realDonaldTrump/status/865173176854204416

Pg 128 *(05/18/17)* https://twitter.com/realDonaldTrump/status/865207118785372160

Pg 129 *(05/19/17)* https://www.whitehouse.gov/briefings-statements/remarks-president-trump-president-santos-colombia-joint-press-conference/

Pg 130 *(05/20/17)* https://twitter.com/realDonaldTrump/status/865865814099939328

Pg 131 *(05/21/17)* http://time.com/4787797/donald-trump-yemen-saudi-arabia-arms-deal/?xid=homepage

Pg 132 *(05/22/17)* https://www.cnn.com/2017/05/21/politics/trump-saudi-speech-transcript/

Pg 133 *(05/23/17)* https://twitter.com/realDonaldTrump/status/867043258932875264

Pg 134 *(05/24/17)* http://www.dailymail.co.uk/news/article-4530634/Trump-visits-Jerusalems-Western-Wall-pray.html

Pg 135 *(05/25/17)* https://twitter.com/realDonaldTrump/status/867354520526872576

Pg 136 *(05/26/17)* https://www.cnn.com/2017/05/25/politics/trump-pushes-prime-minister-nato-summit/

Pg 137 *(05/27/17)* https://www.politicususa.com/2017/05/27/trump-tired-ride-golf-cart-foreign-leaders-walked.html

Pg 138 *(05/28/17)* https://twitter.com/realDonaldTrump/status/868801710038372352

Pg 139 *(05/29/17)* https://www.washingtonexaminer.com/watch-trump-sings-along-to-national-anthem-at-arlington-cemetery/article/2624397

Pg 140 *(05/30/17)* https://www.washingtonpost.com/world/national-security/russian-ambassador-told-moscow-that-kushner-wanted-secret-communications-channel-with-kremlin/2017/05/26/520a14b4-422d-11e7-9869-bac8b446820a_story.html?utm_term=.5aef76dbe123

Pg 141 *(05/31/17)* http://trumptrump.tumblr.com/post/161316445801/despite-the-constant-negative-press-covfefe

Pg 142 *(06/01/17)* https://www.whitehouse.gov/briefings-statements/statement-president-trump-paris-climate-accord/

Pg 143 *(06/02/17)* https://twitter.com/realDonaldTrump/status/870077441401905152

Pg 144 *(06/03/17)* https://twitter.com/realdonaldtrump/status/871325606901895168?lang=en

Pg 145 *(06/04/17)* http://thehill.com/homenews/administration/335453-trump-many-leaks-are-fabricated-lies-made-up-by-fake-news-media

Pg 146 *(06/05/17)* https://www.politifact.com/truth-o-meter/statements/2017/jun/04/donald-trump/donald-trumps-tweet-misleads-about-london-mayors-r/

Pg 147 *(06/06/17)* https://twitter.com/realDonaldTrump/status/871331574649901056

Pg 148 *(06/07/17)* https://twitter.com/realDonaldTrump/status/871674214356484096

Pg 149 *(06/08/17)* https://twitter.com/realDonaldTrump/status/871675245043888128

Pg 150 *(06/09/17)* https://twitter.com/realDonaldTrump/status/871677472202477568 and https://twitter.com/realDonaldTrump/status/871679061847879682

Pg 151 *(06/10/17)* https://www.vox.com/2017/6/7/15758412/comey-testimony-trump-loyalty

Pg 152 *(06/11/17)* https://twitter.com/realDonaldTrump/status/873120139222306817

Pg 153 *(06/12/17)* https://twitter.com/realDonaldTrump/status/873183401620230144

Pg 154 *(06/13/17)* https://www.cnbc.com/2017/06/12/trump-makes-bizarre-claims-at-press-event-as-cabinet-members-take-turns-praising-him.html

Pg 155 *(06/14/17)* https://www.usatoday.com/story/news/politics/onpolitics/2017/06/14/s-president-trumps-71st-birthday/102853306/

Pg 156 *(06/15/17)* https://twitter.com/realDonaldTrump/status/875305788708974592

Pg 157 *(06/16/17)* https://twitter.com/realDonaldTrump/status/875690204564258816

Pg 158 *(06/17/17)* https://twitter.com/realDonaldTrump/status/875321478849363968

Pg 159 *(06/18/17)* https://twitter.com/realDonaldTrump/status/878946025662296064

Pg 160 *(06/19/17)* https://www.washingtonpost.com/politics/trump-vows-insurance-for-everybody-in-obamacare-replacement-plan/2017/01/15/5f2b1e18-db5d-11e6-ad42-f3375f271c9c_story.html

Pg 161 *(06/20/17)* https://www.politico.com/story/2017/03/trump-obamacare-promises-236021

Pg 162 *(06/21/17)* http://www.latimes.com/politics/washington/la-na-essential-washington-updates-trump-says-he-hopes-senate-health-care-1498095617-htmlstory.html

Pg 163-164 *(06/22/17 - 06/23/17)* https://www.businessinsider.com/trump-senate-healthcare-fox-friends-interview-2017-6

Pg 165 *(06/24/17)* https://twitter.com/realDonaldTrump/status/878717095701336064

Pg 166 *(06/25/17)* https://twitter.com/realDonaldTrump/status/879326984794517507

Pg 167 *(06/26/17)* https://twitter.com/realDonaldTrump/status/879315860178993152

Pg 168 *(06/27/17)* https://twitter.com/realDonaldTrump/status/879828637733793793

Pg 169 *(06/28/17)* http://www.foxnews.com/travel/2017/06/28/fake-time-magazine-covers-featuring-donald-trump-found-hanging-in-several-trump-golf-clubs.html

Pg 170 *(06/29/17)* https://twitter.com/realDonaldTrump/status/880408582310776832 and https://twitter.com/realDonaldTrump/status/880410114456465411

Pg 171 *(06/30/17)* https://twitter.com/realDonaldTrump/status/880771685460344832 and https://twitter.com/realDonaldTrump/status/881140479454310401

Pg 172 *(07/01/17)* https://twitter.com/realDonaldTrump/status/881137079958241280

Pg 173 *(07/02/17)* http://www.latimes.com/politics/la-pol-updates-everything-president-july-1499044923-htmlstory.html

Pg 174 *(07/03/17)* https://twitter.com/realDonaldTrump/status/881834692282109953

Pg 175 *(07/04/17)* https://twitter.com/realDonaldTrump/status/881604490041995271

Pg 176 *(07/05/17)* https://www.nytimes.com/2017/07/01/us/politics/trump-epa-chief-pruitt-regulations-climate-change.html?_r=0

Pg 177 *(07/06/17)* https://twitter.com/realDonaldTrump/status/881281755017355264

Pg 178 *(07/07/17)* https://twitter.com/realDonaldTrump/status/884012097805406208

Pg 179 *(07/08/17)* https://twitter.com/realDonaldTrump/status/884374529660903424 and https://twitter.com/realDonaldTrump/status/884378624660582405

Pg 180 *(07/09/17)* https://twitter.com/realDonaldTrump/status/883230130885324802

Pg 181 *(07/10/17)* https://twitter.com/realDonaldTrump/status/883012994145280000

Pg 182 *(07/11/17)* http://thehill.com/homenews/administration/341490-trump-my-son-is-a-high-quality-person-and-i-applaud-his-transparency

Pg 183 *(07/12/17)* https://www.huffingtonpost.com/entry/donald-trump-jr-good-boy_us_5967c98fe4b03389bb16137a

Pg 184 *(07/13/17)* https://twitter.com/realDonaldTrump/status/885109663217352704

Pg 185 *(07/14/17)* https://www.nbcnews.com/politics/politics-news/trump-prays-evangelical-leaders-oval-office-n782321

Pg 186 *(07/15/17)* https://twitter.com/realDonaldTrump/status/886283456644251652

Pg 187 *(07/16/17)* https://twitter.com/realDonaldTrump/status/884033889613828096

Pg 188 *(07/17/17)* https://twitter.com/realDonaldTrump/status/887134287350439936

Pg 189 *(07/18/17)* https://twitter.com/realDonaldTrump/status/887654816507408384

Pg 190 *(07/19/17)* https://www.nytimes.com/2017/07/19/us/politics/trump-interview-transcript.html

Pg 191 *(07/20/17)* https://twitter.com/realDonaldTrump/status/888730468732067841

Pg 192 *(07/21/17)* https://www.nytimes.com/2017/07/19/us/politics/trump-interview-transcript.html

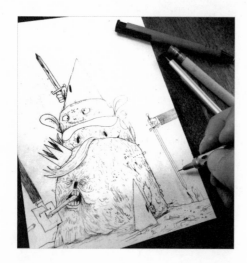

Warren Craghead III lives in Charlottesville, Virginia, USA with his wife and two daughters.

He likes to make pictures and has exhibited his work internationally. He has also published many works including the Xeric Grant winning *Speedy* and several collaborations with poets and writers. He has been nominated for an Ignatz Award and a Pushcart Prize and is a three-time Virginia Museum of Fine Art Fellow.

He received an MFA rom the University of Texas at Austin, a BFA from Virginia Commonwealth University in Richmond, Virginia, and attended the Skowhegan School.

See his work at craghead.com.
See daily updates of Trump drawings at trumptrump.biz.